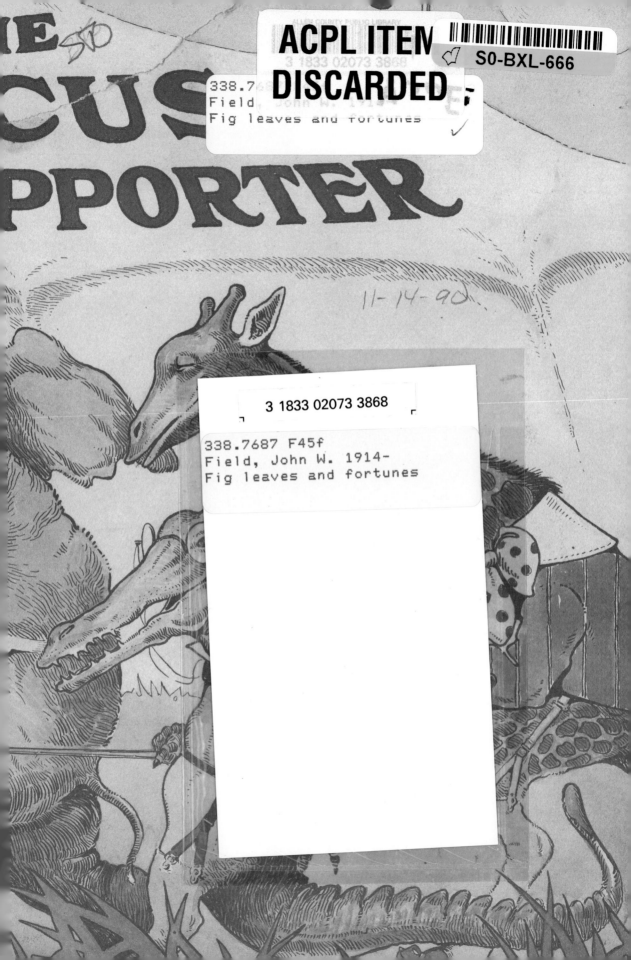

FIG LEAVES AND FORTUNES

FIG LEAVES AN D FORTUNES

a fashion company named

WARNACO

By
John W. Field

PHOENIX PUBLISHING
West Kennebunk, Maine

The following are either trademarks of Warnaco, Inc.,
or proprietary words used by the company in the marketing of its
products: Warner's, LeGant, A'lure, Sta-Up-Top, Stretch-bra,
Half-Size, Merry Widow, Hathaway, Lady Hathaway, Puritan,
Thane, White Stag, Rosanna, and Olga. Speedo and Dior
are used by license from Speedo, Inc., Sydney, Australia,
and Dior from Dior, Paris.

Library of Congress Cataloging-in-Publication Data

Field, John W. (John Warner), 1914—
    Fig leaves and fortunes: the story of a fashion
company named Warnaco / by John W. Field.
        p.   cm.
    ISBN 0-914659-46-4
    1. Warnaco—History. 2. Clothing trade—United
States—History—20th century. 3. Clothing trade—
History—20th century. 4. Fashion merchandising—
United States—History—20th century.
I. Title.
HD9940.U6W374   1990
338.7'687'0973—dc20   90-33520
                                                  CIP

Printed in the United States of America

And the eyes of them both were opened

and they knew that they were naked

and they sewed fig leaves together

and made themselves aprons.

GENESIS:3:7

Contents

For the early days of the doctors Warner I relied on *The Story of My Life* by Lucien Calvin Warner, privately printed in New York in 1914. The archives in the library at Oberlin College, presided over by W.E. Bagglestone, were also a valuable source of information on the Warner family's associations with Oberlin.

Mary Wykowski and the historic collections at the Bridgeport Public Library helped immeasurably with local history and with files of the Warner family, particularly those of D.H. Warner. The staff at the Fairfield Historical Society gave me considerable help as well as information on the Burr Homestead. Frank S. Child's *An Historic Mansion — the Thaddeus Burr Homestead*, published in 1915, was also a source of information. My cousin, Lucetta Warner Clark, kindly loaned me her mother's scrapbook of newspaper articles on D.H. Warner written in the twenties.

On the Field family history I had help from another cousin, Helen Lois Livingston, whose mother was John Field's sister. Helen Lois has long been the family's historian. For Hathaway, I am indebted to *The C.F. Hathaway Company, The First One Hundred and Twenty-Five Years*, published in 1978 as a thesis in Business Administration by Louis L. LaPierre at Thomas College, Waterville, Maine. The rest of the Warnaco story is from *Always Starting Things*, written by Lucien T. Warner in 1944, from company files, my own files, and from personal memory.

Background material on the history of fashion through the years came from *The Pictorial History of Fashion* by Crown Publishers, New York, 1968, from *Victorian and Edwardian Fashions*, by Alison Gersheim, Dover Publications, New York, 1963, from *Lingerie in Vogue, since 1910*, by Christina Probert, Conde Nast, 1981, and from *The Encyclopedia of Fashion* by Georgina O'Hara, Harry N. Abrams, Publishers, 1986.

The quotation from Honore de Balzac in the foreword is from his *Fille d'Eve*, 1839, the quotation from Herbert Norris in chapter three from *Costume and Fashion*, Volume VI, the Nineteenth Century, published in 1933, and the quotation from John Ruskin in chapter four is from his *Fors Clavigera*, 1876.

I am, as always, deeply indebted to my wife, Priscilla, for her help and patience during all the years in which it took to research, remember, and write this family chronicle. It could not have been done without her.

J.W.F.

Foreword

ON FRIDAY, APRIL 25, 1986, the fashion apparel firm, Warnaco, was sold for $487 million. It was the owner of such well-known clothing brands as Warner's, Olga, Hathaway, White Stag, Puritan, and was the largest licensee in the world for Christian Dior of Paris. The purchaser was W. Acquisition Corp., an entrepreneurial company put together by a group of California investors for the sole purpose of making the acquisition.

Compared to the megalithic mergers of those years, the Warnaco take-over was a relatively minor event. The negotiations for the deal, protracted and sometimes bitter, received their share of attention from the financial and apparel press and in the newspapers of localities where Warnaco had brand headquarters, warehouses, or plants. But the world at large little noted, nor, I am sure, long remembered the details.

It seems to me, however, that the story *does* have significance. It is an illustration, particularly poignant for those involved as long-time employees and owners, of how so many American companies, not just the giant firms but the smaller and middle-sized ones too, were being weakened in an era of greed. Facing takeover frenzy fueled by easy money in junk bonds, so many companies, including Warnaco, were being forced to operate, and are operating today, under larger and larger debt loads. It is the story of a company that culminated in the takeover, but had its roots in the past, as generation after generation of managers struggled to guide it through increasingly perilous, and confusing, times.

Of particular importance also is the fact that Warnaco is a fashion company. Fashions reflect the history and life-styles of a people. Men, women, and children reveal who they are and what they want to be by the clothes they wear. Balzac once wrote that a woman's way of dressing is "a permanent revelation of her most secret thoughts, a language and a symbol," and that "dress is a sort of symbolic language, the study of which it would be madness to neglect." The story of Warnaco is thus not only a story of a company, but a study of fashion and of history. In 1986 Warnaco, including its original company, Warner's, was 112 years old (its Hathaway division was 150 years old), having lived through

Lucien C. Warner

I. DeVer Warner

DeVer H. Warner

John Field

more than a century of history, designing fashions for a country and a world in constant change. History, fashion, and Warnaco marched hand-to-hand through those years.

In other ways too the Warnaco story is a fascinating, though maybe not unique, saga. It is the story of two ambitious young doctors founding a business, seeing it grow and prosper, passing it on to succeeding generations, each new one with new ideas and new ambitions, and often scorn for the old. It is a story of those men and women who in their time ran the company, their strengths, their weaknesses, their successes, their failures, their all too human foibles. And it is a story, in the end, of a family losing the game and the sadness of surrendering to strangers.

John W. Field

Fairfield, Connecticut
May, 1990

John W. Field *James C. Walker* *Robert J. Matura* *Linda J. Wachner*

FIG LEAVES AND FORTUNES

1

Before 1866

T WAS AUGUST 1860. Secession of the southern states and a civil war were looming ever closer. Abraham Lincoln, as the candidate of the Republicans, was running for the presidency against Stephen Douglas, candidate of the northern Democrats, and John Breckinridge, candidate of the southern Democrats. Already the South was threatening to leave the Union if Lincoln became president. An Atlanta newspaper wrote, "Whether the Potomac is crimsoned with human gore and Pennsylvania Avenue is paved ten fathoms deep with mangled bodies, or whether the last vestige of liberty is swept from the face of the American continent, the South will never submit to such humiliation and degradation as the inauguration of Abraham Lincoln."

In Paris another newspaper reported a tragedy. A young lady whom all her rivals had admired for her tiny waist, was dead two days after a ball. What had happened? Her family wanted to know what had caused her sudden death at "such an early age, and it was decided to perform an autopsy. The result was shattering: the liver had been pierced by three ribs! This is how one dies at 23 years old! Not of typhus, not in childbirth, but of a corset!"

On an early morning in that summer month of August a wagon slipped out of a tiny farm in the hamlet of Lincklaen in central New York state. The village, situated in the valley of Mud Creek, contained thirty inhabitants as well as a tavern, a blacksmith shop, a shoemaker, a post office, a small general store, and a Congregational church. The farm, of about twenty acres, had been purchased some years before by a Mrs. Lydia Ann Converse Warner who lived there alone with her two sons, Ira DeVer and Lucien. Her father had boarded with her for some years before 1860 but he had a predilection for tippling and life was easier for Mrs. Warner after he departed this world. It had been embarrassing for her when he raided the produce cellar for apples and potatoes and sold them to the innkeeper for whiskey.

As a matter of fact, Mrs. Warner had been unfortunate with the other men in her life too. Her father-in-law was killed by a horse which kicked him in the head, and her husband died when the children were very young. He was not a good business man and often traded horses with other men and always got the worst of the bargain.

As a result Mrs. Warner had full responsibility for running the farm and raising the children. Years later her son, Lucien, would describe life in Lincklaen. "It was only the hard work and good management of my mother that held the family together. Most of our food was raised on the place, except flour and groceries, and these were provided from the sale of the butter we made. We rarely had any meat except cold pork and occasional fowl when there was company. We also had salted codfish and mackerel and an occasional trout or catfish caught from the local stream. . . . The total amount of money spent by the family during the year, except for the barest necessities, would not exceed three dollars."

Even news from the outside world took a long time to reach the valley. Lucien wrote, "I do not remember that any magazine came into my hands and very few papers of any kind. A few of our neighbors took the *Weekly Tribune*. My uncle took Moore's *Rural New Yorker* and my aunt took the *Female Guardian*, a paper published in the interests of the New York Home for the Friendless. A cousin of mine took the *New York Ledger*, but she was thought to be rather worldly-minded. The ten-cent paper-covered novel then took the place of the cheap present magazine stories. These gave a vivid description of life as it does not exist except in a diseased imagination, but through some good fortune I escaped the contamination of this unwholesome literature."

Both the brothers disliked farm life and resolved to escape from it as soon as they could. Lucien wrote, "There is no variety or inspiration in hoeing a long row of corn or potatoes. Each hill is the exact duplicate of its fellow. . . . Pulling weeds in the garden was even worse, for the weeds and the young beets and carrots all looked so much alike that I could never tell them apart, and working on my hands and knees always gave me a backache."

What the boys did enjoy was the one-room schoolhouse located about a mile north of their home. There they walked every school day, through the blizzards of winter, the rains of spring, the heat of summer, and the glories of a northern autumn. Lucien was the smaller of the two, the more studious and intellectual, DeVer the larger, more extroverted and gregarious. They were both musically talented and attended the country "singing school," which met regularly during the winter months. There they learned harmony, and DeVer taught himself to play the melodeon and the violin. To his own accompaniment (and his own pleasure) he enlivened many a long winter night with his singing of the popular songs of the day. This talent was to stand him in good stead when some years later he became a traveling lecturer and sometime troubador.

In those days, for boys who did not want to remain on the farm, the principal avenue of escape was to teach school. DeVer was the first to try it in the winter of 1856-57 when he was sixteen years old. He taught at a small backwoods community called Stoney Brook, two miles from their home. The next year when he fell ill, Lucien substituted for him and received sixteen dollars a month for his amateur efforts.

But teaching local schools, the boys felt, was a poor substitute for the marvels of an outside world where one could be part of the rush and turmoil of a growing, vigorous, but currently troubled, nation. As schoolboys and local teachers they never ventured beyond the few miles surrounding their farm, and they were part of a small, isolated, rural community. They wanted more.

Lucien's deliverance came in the form of a Reverend Shubael Carver, graduate of the Oberlin (Ohio) Theological Seminary and teacher at an academy in nearby DeRuyter. Lucien described the Reverend Carter as "a born teacher and inspirer of young men and women. . . . He put us in touch with the life and spirit of the outside world, and led us to see that there were conquests to be made and responsibilities to be met outside of the quiet valley in which we lived." It was through the Reverend Carter that Lucien received a scholarship at Oberlin College which gave him free tuition. It was assumed that he could earn enough by working to pay for his board, clothing, books, and expenses.

And so it was on that late summer day of 1860 that Lucien Warner, accompanied by the Reverend Carter, left his quiet valley in the farm wagon. The way from Lincklaen to Oberlin in those days was a long one. They drove the farm wagon as far as Apulia, New York, where they boarded the railroad, newly built, for Syracuse. Here they changed cars and went by the New York Central to Buffalo. Because there were no through trains west, it was necessary to continue by steamship and spend the night on Lake Erie before disembarking the next morning at Cleveland to take another train for Oberlin. Lucien wrote, "I had never been away from home before and was now seeing the world. I was astonished at the immense buildings in Syracuse and Buffalo and the First Church of Oberlin was the largest audience room I had ever seen."

Oberlin College was very much a part of the outside world, a remarkable institution for its times. One of the very first liberal arts colleges to enroll women as full-time students, it had also attracted, accepted, and sheltered black students, many of them refugees from the South. Abolitionist sentiment ran high on the campus. When anti-slavery agitation was banned at Lake Theological Seminary in Cincinnati, virtually the entire student body transferred to Oberlin.

In the halls and classrooms of such an institution the nation's problems were ever present. It cheered when Lincoln was elected president in November. It watched with apprehension as eleven southern states, led by South Carolina, seceded from the Union. It was encouraged by Lincoln's inaugural address on March 4, 1861, when he spoke to the South: "In your hands, my dissatisfied fellow countrymen, and not in mine, is the momentous issue of civil war . . . no state, on its own mere action, can get out of the Union." And it exploded in a wave of excitement when South Carolina military forces fired on Fort Sumter in April and the war was on.

Lucien Warner wrote his brother: "It is in the midst of the most intense and alarming excitement that I address you these lines. WAR! . . . and volunteers are the only topic of conversation or thought. The lessons of today have been a mere form. I cannot study; I cannot sleep; I cannot work; and I don't know as I can write. It is no longer secession but civil war. No longer keep the southern states in the Union, but protect and preserve the liberties of the country."

Lucien's first impulse was to join the rush to enroll in the army. But objectivity prevailed. He explained, "The one fixed purpose of my life was to get a college education and to enter the Army at that time would have been to abandon this purpose." Besides, he was finding it harder than he had expected to earn money and he was working more hours in a week than he was devoting to his studies in order to be able to pay his expenses. He was doing any kind of job he could find: repairing locks and door handles, setting glass, papering rooms, digging trenches, laying tiles. His expenses at Oberlin for the first full year were $160. Of this he earned $75 in manual labor. Later, as he advanced into the upper academic forms, he was able to support himself by teaching.

Before 1866

Even in those early days Lucien was showing a concern for order and sobriety, a fondness for quiet living, good reading, pleasant conversation, that were to mark his later years. He did not enjoy the rough and tumble of purely masculine companionship. Of his "club" where he boarded at the cost of one dollar a week, he wrote his mother, "The club is composed of fourteen young men . . . such a collection of boarders is just what could be expected from a lot of young men living excluded from ladies. Some . . . only wish to swallow their food and run. Without the restraining and refining influence of ladies, it is impossible to maintain decorum."

It was therefore with considerable pleasure that he shifted to the Ladies Hall where his board went up to $1.37 a week, but the company was an improvement. From there he wrote his brother, "I enjoy boarding at the Hall very much. I sit at one of the best tables and have for a table mate one of the finest and smartest ladies in the Hall. I never knew a person whose conversation was so interesting and profitable as hers. She has travelled considerable [sic] and can converse on any subject."

Poor Lucien! Later in life he could not even remember the lady's name.

In the fall of 1862 Lucien interrupted his studies, which consisted mostly of Greek, Latin, and mathematics (no English, almost no history), to return home for the winter. During his two-year absence there had been important family changes. His mother, desperately lonely, had married a Quaker named William Breed. Neither Lucien nor his brother appears to have been overly fond of their new step-father. Lucien described him as a man of "narrow views and penurious habits." Later, when the fortunes of both Lucien and DeVer had improved, they tried to relieve the poverty of the aging couple but "we found it displeased our step-father and so brought no happiness to our mother."

Lucien's brother had also changed the course of his life. He had abandoned any plans he might have harbored for college and instead had entered medical school at Geneva Medical College in Geneva, New York. In those days one did not need a college degree to become a doctor. He graduated as validictorian of his class, settled down in Nineveh, New York, and married Lucetta M. Greenman, of McGrawville, New York. Soon he would move to McGrawville with his bride and buy out the practice of a certain Dr. Kingman, thus settling into the career of a small town doctor. During the next couple of years he became the father of two children, Annie Lucetta and DeVer Howard. In both Nineveh and McGrawville, whenever Lucien was home from college, he would spend many weeks at his brother's home, and together they would ponder and plan their futures long into the night.

But no matter how concerned a young man was with his own future, no one in the years 1861-65 could escape the fervor of the Civil War. At Oberlin almost everybody served at one time or another in the army. Lucien's first experience with the military had elements of comedy. The Confederates were threatening Cincinnati, and all loyal Ohioans were rushing to their Queen City's rescue. Lucien described what happened. "A company was made up of the students at Oberlin, which I joined. We had no uniforms and no ordinary marksmen's rifles, and knew almost nothing about using these. But we rushed on to Cincinnati and were welcomed by the frightened citizens with open arms and free lunches. By the time we were in the city the Confederates were in full retreat and at the end of the week we were back at our studies." Each member of the company received a certificate for bravery.

Not so inconsequential was his second spell in the army. In early July 1864 Confederate forces under General Jubal Early had raided Maryland and were headed for Washington. A demand went out for volunteers to man the forts around the Capitol, most of the seasoned troops being off with General Grant moving on Richmond. In response Lucien joined a company of students from Oberlin. With no training they went to Cleveland and were mustered into the army as Company K of the 150th Regiment of Ohio Volunteers. Lucien himself was put in charge of a cannon firing an eight-inch shell.

Lucien recalled vividly the trip to Washington. "At Pittsburgh we left the train and marched up into a large city hall, where the ladies of the city served us with a nice free luncheon. From there on, our trip was in freight cars. It was very hot, and I remember riding on top of the cars and sleeping through the long tunnel at the summit of the Allegheny Range."

In Washington Lucien saw President Lincoln at close-hand. General Early's attack on the city was momentarily expected, and Fort Stevens, where Lucien was stationed, was to be the center of the attack. On Sunday July 10 the president came to the fort. "I remember distinctly his tall, gaunt form, his long, yellowish coat, and his strong, kindly face as he returned our salute and took a position quite near my gun," wrote Lucien. The next day, in the midst of Early's assault, Lincoln came again. "His tall form attracted the attention of the enemy, and the bullets began to whizz over our heads with increasing frequency. Soon a surgeon in the President's party was wounded by a bullet in his leg and was carried to the rear. President Lincoln then . . . retired from his exposed position."

Company K could not retire. In spite of their lack of training, the men fought well. Lucien wrote, "A large number (of Confederate soldiers) stole up behind a fine house about a half mile in front of us, and from there the sharpshooters were picking off our men. At the word of command, we concentrated the fire of our cannon on this house, and in less than ten minutes it was a mass of flames. . . . At the onset (of the main Southern attack) our fort joined in with cannon and musketry, but in less than five minutes the lines had met, and nothing was to be seen but a single cloud of smoke, out of which came a continual roar of musketry. The bullets passed over us like a shower of hail. . . . In about half an hour the Confederates gave way, and the day was won. . . . A few burned houses and scarred trees and three hundred and seventy three dead and wounded soldiers in an improvised hospital just back of our fort were all that was left to show that Washington had barely escaped pillage and destruction."

Victory achieved, Company K returned to Cleveland and to school, having served one hundred and sixteen days.

During the following winter Lucien visited his brother at McGrawville and taught at the district school. It was in retrospect a memorable winter for it was then that he met Karen Osborne, his future wife. In his autobiography he solemnly reported . . . "She was a tall, slim girl of fifteen, bright in conversation, popular in society, and of attractive personality. Afterwards I saw her from time to time when I was in McGrawville, but it was nearly three years later that the friendship developed into that stronger feeling which has united our lives for over forty years."

Meanwhile Lucien had things other than love on his mind, most important being to complete the last six months of college. He had hardly returned to Oberlin in the spring of 1865 when Petersburg and then Richmond fell to General Grant, and the war was over. Along with the whole North, Oberlin exploded in ecstasy only to be suddenly shocked just a few days later by the news of Lincoln's death. Lucien wrote his mother, "The past week our studies have been greatly interrupted by rejoicing and mourning. All business was suspended . . . and in Cleveland nearly everyone rejoiced by getting drunk, but we remained sober and rejoiced. . . . [Then] we received the news of the assassination of President Lincoln. It was as though a clap of thunder had stunned every person. The news was brought to our class at the close of a recitation. For nearly five minutes we sat motionless, forgetting that the class had been dismissed. I have loved other public men, but the death of no one could have affected me like that of President Lincoln. Ever since I looked upon his honest, genial countenance I have loved him like an intimate friend; and so, I suppose, did every loyal man."

As Andrew Johnson took over the presidency and Lincoln's killer, John Wilkes Booth, was shot to death near Bowling Green, Virginia, life at Oberlin returned to a form of normalcy. Lucien's oration at the commencement exercises on August 24 was on the "Conservation and Correlation of Force," and treated the fact that heat, electricity, and motion were all interchangeable. He commented that this abstruse topic was "probably an indication of the natural bent of my mind toward scientific and mechanical subjects."

Commencement marked the end of Lucien's days as a student at Oberlin, but in reality it was just the beginning of his lifetime association with his college. He recalled, "No part of my whole life is so indelibly impressed on my mind as my school days at Oberlin, and no part has had so large an influence in forming my character and shaping my future life. No friends that I have ever made have been so dear to me as those I made during my college days . . . the debt of obligation I owe to my beloved teachers, I can never repay."

Oberlin itself was to be eternally grateful that Lucien C. Warner had once been a student there.

Warner Concert Hall at Oberlin College given in memory of Lucien C. Warner in 1963.

2

1866 - 1874

THE YEARS AFTER the Civil War constituted a tragic era in American history. The news reported the pains of reconstruction in the South, the franchising and sufferings of the blacks, the days of the scalawags and carpetbaggers, the theatrics of the Ku Klux Klan, the great Chicago fire, the impeachment trial of Andrew Johnson, the election of General Grant as president and the scandals that followed, the speculations of Jim Fisk and Jay Gould, and the venomous presidential campaign of 1872 when Horace Greeley went down to defeat as Grant, in spite of the scandals, was reelected. Greeley, subject of venomous vilification, said, "I hardly knew whether I was running for the presidency or the penitentiary."

In Paris, London, New York, and other social centers women leaders of fashion were wearing enormous flounced crinolines and hooped skirts, yards wide, many requiring up to 180 feet of wire to hold them out. The waist was as small as the bones of the corset could make it, the deep decollete of the tight, uplifted bodice leaving the upper part of the breasts, the shoulders, and the arms bare.

But something far more important than politics or fashion was happening to the United States: industrialization. Before the war the country had been a nation of small farms and small towns, just the kind of place where the Warner family lived. The change from a nation based on farming to one dependent on industry might have come about anyway, but it was immeasurably hastened by the miraculous inventions of the century and by the arrival of millions of immigrants from Europe and Asia to provide inexpensive labor. In rapid succession the inventions came: electricity, the telephone, the calculating machine, the mechanical reaper, the Bessemer steel process, the telegraph, the Kodak camera, the rotary printing press, the steam engine, and most important for the future of the doctors Warner, the sewing machine. Such inventions propelled the rush to build intercontinental railroads, steel mills, petroleum refineries, flour mills, glass furnaces, and automated slaughterhouses. A befuddled visitor from Scotland wrote from Chicago in 1868 that he had seen a slaughterhouse in which a pig was converted from an "intelligent pig on the gangway into pork, packed in barrels, and ready for shipment," all in twelve minutes. The heroes of the day were men like James T. Hill, Leland Stanford, Andrew Carnegie, and John D. Rockefeller, who in the years ahead was to be a close friend of Dr. I. DeVer Warner. To man the vast enterprises which these and other business leaders built, the immigrants were just the thing. Thousands of Chinese were imported to build the railroads; by 1875 almost one-fifth of America's population was foreign born.

The brothers, I. DeVer and Lucien Warner, were caught up in all this. Perhaps it was the deprivations of their boyhoods; more likely it was simply the spirit of the times. After the national idealism of the Civil War, materialism ran rampant: everybody wanted to get rich quick, and the Warners were no exception. However, when Lucien left Oberlin in 1865, business and businessmen were still not highly respected, at least not in educated circles, and as he explained, "To a college graduate . . . the choice of deciding what his life work would be was practically limited to one of the four professions: teaching, the ministry, medicine, and law." The one thing both of them knew was that they did not want to be farmers.

The choice for DeVer appears to have been easy. Not being a college graduate, he chose medicine, which after a few years, if something more lucrative came along, he was prepared to abandon. As events were to prove, he was a born entrepreneur. The choice was harder for the more intellectual Lucien. Having no taste for the ministry in spite of deep religious beliefs, having tired of teaching, and thinking he was too poor a public speaker for the law, he settled without real conviction on medicine. The fact that his brother was already a successful doctor undoubtedly influenced him. In October of 1865, having spent a few weeks visiting DeVer in McGrawville, he set out for New York City and the Medical Department of New York University. A scholarship required him to pay only fifty dollars a year tuition.

Lucien loved New York, an affection he was to keep the rest of his life. He was at home with the action and intensity of the city. He made many new friends, among them, Peter Cooper, aging but still dynamic, the builder of the "Tom Thumb" locomotive, originator of the Canton Iron Works, a supporter of Cyrus Field's Atlantic cable, president of the North American Telegraph Company, a millionaire, and founder of the Cooper Union for the Advancement of Science and Art. Cooper was a prototype of the kind of new industrialist and philanthropist America was producing, and a man whom an impressionable Lucien Warner could take as a model.

In the early spring of 1866, after scarcely a few months at medical school, Lucien, needing money, returned home. There in an old wagon, pulled by a partly broken colt, he traveled to the neighboring town of Freetown where he set himself up as a practicing country doctor, his medical inventory consisting of a few simple medicines and tools of the trade including forceps for pulling teeth. He wrote, "My books show that I treated over sixty patients in seven months. . . . Such an act would probably now be illegal, but at that time no objection seemed to be made. Fortunately, as far as I can judge, no one was made worse by my immature medical skills."

Meanwhile his brother, DeVer, was continuing as a doctor in McGrawville, ambitious to find something better, or at least something more remunerative. It was at this time that both young men, almost simultaneously, came up with the idea which was to dramatically change their lives. The idea was simple enough, certainly not revolutionary even then.

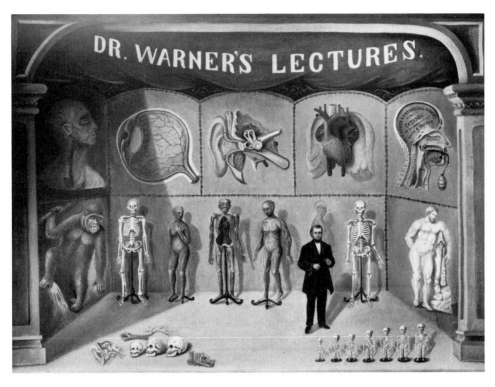

Artist's rendering of Dr. I. DeVer Warner lecturing on anatomy, circa 1868-69.

Lucien expressed it: "The greater part of the sickness the physician is called upon to treat is preventable, and the chief need of the world is not more physicians but more knowledge of the laws of health." In other words, if you learn how to lead a healthy life, you will avoid much illness. The popularity of this idea was demonstrated by a lecture DeVer gave on how to lead such a life before the New York Central Academy in McGrawville. The lecture was a resounding success, even if the lecturer was not exactly an expert on the subject.

Stimulated by this success, the brothers decided to give a series of lectures on psychology and hygiene, charging admission fees. During the next winter, while Lucien completed his medical studies in New York, they made their preparations. From his school's dissecting room Lucien purloined a real hand, foot, and heart. Together they purchased a skeleton, a life-size manikin, and a large collection of maps and charts of the human body along with skulls and other props with the idea of mesmerizing, and possibly enlightening, their audiences, while at the same time strengthening their bank accounts. When finished, the stage setting for their lectures bore a fascinating resemblance to the settings of the American Museum in New York owned by the circus-man, P.T. Barnum, later to be their friend in Bridgeport, Connecticut. That museum too featured skeletons, waxwork figures, and stuffed animals.

The lectures, which proved popular and profitable, began in 1867 and continued for several years, presented mostly in small towns in New York, Pennsylvania, and Ohio. DeVer

1866 - 1874

was the better speaker, often enlivening the procedings by tunes on his mandolin, while Lucien was the better writer. Lucien commented, "My brother had a marked gift as a public speaker and when we secured a good audience the first night of our scheduled series of lectures, we seldom failed to hold it to the end of the course. . . . He had a keen sense of humor which kept the audience both interested and pleased. . . . For this reason it gradually came about that my brother did most of the lecturing and I attended to the advertising and business management." This division of labor was to continue throughout their careers.

Even Lucien's marriage to Karen Osborne in the fall of 1867 did not interrupt the lecture tours. Lucien wrote, "After our marriage my wife usually traveled with me and assisted in various ways in running the business. Her special part was selling tickets for twenty-five cents each, while I took them up at the door. My brother's wife was also with us part of the time and sometimes had with her one or both of their young children. In this way we made quite a family party, usually all stopping at the same hotel."

The lectures were proving so successful and the idea of preventive medicine so financially rewarding that the brothers' imaginative minds jumped to other ventures. When on tour they advertised office hours during the day while awaiting their nightly performances. Their patients suffered mostly from "chronic diseases such as dyspepsia, rheumatism, catarrh, and nervous complaints." They were especially successful in treating catarrh. Lucien explained, "My brother and I invented a syringe for treating catarrh by injecting medicines from the back part of the throat through the nasal cavities, the liquid being discharged from the nose. It was known as Dr. Warner's catarrhal douche and was sold in the leading drugstores of the country." Alongside it stood bottles of "Warner's Safe Cure: For Kidney and Liver, Bright's Disease; Urinary Disorders; Female Complaints; General Debility. Malaria, and all diseases caused by disordered kidneys and liver."

Next came the medical books, written by the brothers, which still can be found in libraries across the country. The first, by Lucien, was titled the *Functions and Diseases of Women* and was really a discreet sex manual. The book was sold in connection with the lectures and by canvassing agents secured through ads in *Harper's Weekly*. Lucien reported that the book received "very flattering testimonials as to its clearness and style and the chaste way in which it treated of delicate matters." It sold 7,000 copies, a big sale in those days.

The second book, *Man in Health and Disease* was a collaborative effort by the two brothers, with DeVer preparing the research and Lucien doing the writing and editing. It was not as successful as the first book, Lucien admitting rather wanly that "the demand for a book for men proved to be rather smaller than for the book for women." It sold only 2,500 copies.

By the winter of 1872-73 the partnership of the brothers on the lecture circuit and the nomadic life were wearing thin. DeVer retreated to his practice in McGrawville, only occasionally giving lectures, while Lucien, now encumbered by his first child, Agnes, decided to set up a medical practice in New York City. He thought that the reputation he had earned through his books would bring him a paying practice wherever he might locate, and he loved New York.

He was wrong. New York in early September 1873 was struggling through the beginning of the great Panic, in which 5,000 businesses would fail in the first year alone. It was in no mood to be hospitable, or even receptive, to a young, unknown, and inexperienced

Fig Leaves and Fortunes

doctor, his wife, and little baby. Setting up residence and office in a second-floor apartment at 749 Sixth Avenue near 42nd street, he waited for patients who never came. In desperation, thinking that the problem was the second-floor office, he moved to a low basement on 41st street with the idea of renting furnished rooms in other sections of the four-floor building which he purchased. He rented the rooms, all right, but to scoundrels who never paid their bills and wrecked the building. Worse yet, the patients still did not come. He reported, "I do not think I had six patients. One lady to whom I paid many visits moved away without paying my bill." His total income from his medical practice in a year was under two hundred dollars.

Lucien, however, was a patient soul, and short of starvation, he refused to worry. A solution would come. "I did not get discouraged over the medical practice," he philosophized. "In fact I rarely get discouraged over anything. At the end of the first year events occurred which changed the whole course of my future life. The day of waiting for patients who did not come was over, and although I did not immediately abandon the practice of medicine, I was soon so absorbed in the new work that I hardly had time to remember that my doctor's sign was still on the front door."

Warner's Safe Kidney and Liver Cure was prescribed for Bright's disease, urinary disorders, female complaints, neural debility and malaria, not to mention all other diseases caused by disordered kidneys and liver.

1866 - 1874

3

1874 - 1888

POLITICS WERE CORRUPT, the bosses in charge, the new business entrepreneurs intolerant and greedy, labor exploited, but American industry, recovering from the Panic of 1873, was booming. To the great Centennial Exposition in Philadelphia in 1876 came millions of sightseers from all over the world to celebrate the country's 100th birthday. Center of the stage were the American inventions of the last decade, symbolizing, it seemed to some, the rampant materialism of a confident and brash nation. Perhaps the nation did have reason to be confident and brash. Within a generation it would become the world's greatest industrial economy.

A young Englishman named Charles Frederick Worth came to Paris knowing no French and with 117 francs in his pocket. With enormous energy and talent and the help of an attractive young wife, by the 1860s and 1870s he had become the most famous fashion designer in the world and the founder of the French Haute Couture. He was the father of the crinoline and when that style faded, as all styles do, he created the bustle, considered by many an even more outrageous fashion. Observing the bustled dresses on English women in Constantinople, a Turkish lady asked the British Ambassador's wife, "Are all the ladies in your country deformed?"

The bustle still required a wasp waist and uplifted bust provided by a tight, boned corset. Photographic historian Alison Gernsheim in her book *Victorian and Edwardian Fashion* comments, "It was not only a matter of the corset crushing the body; the internal organs were forced permanently out of position — the lower ribs, too, grew quite out of place and stuck into the lungs." Herbert Norris in *Costume and Fashion* acidly added, "At no period in the history of costume have the clothes of men and women been so supremely hideous as those generally worn during the sixties and seventies of the nineteenth century."

Lucien Warner, still a practicing doctor, concurred with the idea of the evils of corsetry. "An entire revolution in woman's dress is greatly needed. A prominent fault is compression of the waist. It is our firm belief that the only really healthful apparel is a loose dress.

12

No tight-fitting dress will permit easy bending and twisting of the body. An evil still more difficult to obviate is that of wearing the under-clothing suspended around the hips. It is of first importance that the weight of the clothing should be borne wholly by the shoulders; for if suspended around the body, not only does their weight fall directly on the bowels and crowd upon the womb, but this steady pressure weakens the muscles of the abdomen. The effect of corsets is to weaken the part which they pretend to support."

The doctors Warner, true to their newly aroused interest in the laws of health and always desirous of making a little more money, looked for something to take the place of a corset yet something which would give all the appearance of a small waist, but not constrict it in an unhealthy way. With this idea in mind, for several years they had carried on their lecture tours a waist pattern to be worn in place of a corset, and this pattern had been copied by several thousand women in the towns they visited. Its problem was that, while it may have been healthy enough, it did little to shape a small waist.

In the summer of 1874 DeVer Warner, full of excitement, wrote his brother that he had found what he was looking for. The revolution against corsetry was at hand. He had invented an improved version of their waist with straps over the shoulders and a projection of cloth held out by a reed at the bottom. In this way he could support the clothing from the shoulders and at the same time, by means of the projecting cloth, give the effect of a small waist without compressing it. He had taken a yard of cloth and his pattern to Moses G. Smith, village postmaster in McGrawville and sometime tailor. Mr. Smith had made up a garment and tried it on his wife who was exuberant in her praise of its comfort and stylish look. DeVer had a few more of these novel corset-waists made up and sent to Lucien in New York. In the city Lucien was in touch with the markets for buying material and selling goods, and DeVer asked him to join him as a partner in distributing the new product through canvassing agents and by displaying them at his lectures. Lucien was at first hesitant, but his medical practice in New York was going nowhere so he thought he could fill his idle time by selling the corset-waists in connection with the sale of his medical books. Any doubts about the saleability of the new product was eliminated when, on his way to a trustee meeting at Oberlin College (he had been elected an Oberlin trustee some time before, and was to continue as such for over fifty years), he stopped off at Painesville Ohio, and there sold three dozen of the new contraptions to a local retailer. He also gave samples to the sixty or so agents, mostly women, who were selling his books, and they were equally enthusiastic and immediately began pushing the product.

Their whatever-it-was, more than a waist, not quite a corset, was an immediate, roaring success. The first goods were made in a single-room tailor shop, under twenty-five feet square, on the unpaved Main Street of McGrawville. The only capital put into the business was $2,550, all further funds to develop it being taken out of profits. Within a few weeks the brothers had a flourishing enterprise on their hands, and both, with considerable relief, gave up their lecturing and medical practices to devote full time to it. If truth were known, neither of them had been very fond of medicine anyway, nor probably very good at it.

Problems, of course, came along with success. They had admittedly copied part of their original garment from one made by a Madame Foy, who threatened to sue. A dexterous change in construction (by dropping the projecting ring at the bottom and substituting brass hooks to which skirts could be attached) eliminated the enfringement and also improved the product. Their first name, "Dr. Warner's Sanitary Corset" was owned by some-

DR. WARNER'S

SANITARY CORSET,

WITH SKIRT SUPPORTER AND SELF-ADJUSTING PADS.

This Corset is constructed upon strictly physiological principles, and while it preserves the beauty and grace of the form better than most other corsets, it does so without the least injury to health or comfort. We would particularly call attention to the following advantages:

1st. It affords a convenient and efficient support for the undercloth-ing. This is very important, for the weight of the clothing crowding down upon the bowels is one of the most frequent causes of the weakness so prevalent among women. Some corsets support the clothing behind and not in front; but this is worse than no support, as it only increases the pressure in front.

2d. The Self-Adjusting Pads are the delight of every lady who tries them. They give elegence to the form, are cool and comfortable, require no adjusting, and never get out of place.

3d. The Corset is made short in front, being but little longer than the dress waist. This allows greater freedom in the movements of the body, and when a lady becomes accustomed to it, is more comfortable. It also avoids the pressure upon the stomach and bowels which is the especial evil of the ordinary corset.

4th. It combines three garments in one, a corset, a skirt supporter, and self-adjusting pads, and yet costs no more than a simple corset made of equally good material and workmanship.

In ordering the Sanitary Corset give the measure around the waist in inches. Four of the accompanying rings should be sewed to the bands of each of the skirts. When a Bustle is worn it should be attached to the hooks upon the back side of the Corset.

MANUFACTURED BY

WARNER BROS., 119 W. 41st Street, New York City.

The first Warner's corset ad ran in 1874. The name was soon changed to Dr. Warner's Health Corset.

Fig Leaves and Fortunes

The table on which the first Warner's corset was cut in McGraw, N.Y. in 1874.

body else, so they had to change to "Dr. Warner's Health Corset," a notable improvement. They also had initial difficulty with the patterns which did not fit as well as they should, neither brother having had any experience in pattern-making. Lucien solved this problem by personally studying pattern-making and becoming his own expert on patterns and grading of sizes. This enabled DeVer in McGrawville, where production was located, to think up new designs (he was the more inventive of the two) while Lucien (the more methodical) in New York made them fit correctly. Lucien also developed a sales organization, selling at first through canvassing agents and then in the second year, directly to retailers.

In that first year of 1874 the business was conducted entirely out of Lucien Warner's home on 41st Street. There the corsets were sent from McGrawville to be ironed and eyeletted, and lace sewed around the top. There too Lucien's wife, Karen, supervised this work and did a good part of the labor herself, on at least one occasion punching a hole completely through the soft end of her finger with an eyelet machine. Even after the business was moved out of their home to a loft on Broadway in the fall of 1875, Karen Warner continued to supervise the finishing department and conducted most of the correspondence with the selling agents.

A prominent weekly, the *New York Independent*, wondered why Dr. Warner's corsets were selling so fast. It concluded that the Health Corsets were fitted to the natural human form, thus being "without detriment to health and comfort." Most important, they made it possible to support the weight of the skirts from the shoulders, not from the waist.

So rapidly were sales increasing that by the spring of 1876, less than two years after the start of the business, the small plant at McGrawville had become hopelessly inadequate, and it was obvious that the manufacturing operations would have to be moved to

1874 - 1888

The first Warner's factory in McGraw, N.Y., 1874-75.

Fig Leaves and Fortunes

The first Warner's factory building in Bridgeport was built in 1876. The men at the extreme right in the top hats are the cutters.

much larger quarters where transportation was better and labor more available. Thus it was, after considerable examination of towns near New York City, that DeVer and Lucien decided on Bridgeport, Connecticut. There in the summer of 1876 they built a brick building on Lafayette Street, forty by one hundred feet, four stories high, and occupied it in the fall. DeVer moved his home, his family, and some of his factory employees to Bridgeport. Warner Brothers has been there ever since.

In the 1870s Bridgeport was a prototype of the new cities growing up with the new industrialization. When the doctors Warner moved there, the city was already a thriving industrial center. It had a superb location on Long Island Sound with a good harbor and a magnificent park, new railroad facilities connecting it with New York, Boston, and interior Hartford, and most important, adequate and inexpensive labor with additional eager European immigrants arriving daily. Its major product, vital for Warners, was sewing machines. Other industries included hats, shirts, toys, furniture, carriages, and saddles. But its most famous business was the circus and its best-known local resident, Phineas T. Barnum, whose Winter Quarters was a distinctive feature of the city down near the railroad tracks. In the Bridgeport of those days one could encounter Tom Thumb or Livinia Warren in a local market, Jenny Lind on a streetcar, see the Tall Man or the Fat Lady strolling down Main Street, meet "Wild Bill" Cody in Seaside Park, or even watch an elephant plowing the Barnum farmlands. When fire broke out some years later, one might have had to dodge escaped elephants, tigers, and lions in back alleys. The year the Warner plant opened, P.T. Barnum was the mayor of Bridgeport, leading a campaign against drunkenness and

1874 - 1888

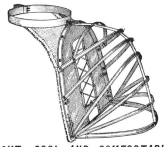

LIGHT, COOL AND COMFORTABLE.

The best Fifty Cent Folding Bustle in the market. It is recommended by fashionable ladies and leading dressmakers. PERFECT in shape and ADJUSTABLE in size. The improved folding principle used in this Bustle results in its always regaining its shape after pressure. It is the easiest and yet the most effective and durable spring ever presented. Its superior finish and elegant style make it a most desirable Bustle.

Warner's version of Taylor's folding bustle which folded up when the wearer sat down.

advocating the closing of all saloons on Sunday. Quite conscious of the deserved reputation of most American politicians for corruption, he spoke to the common council about the honesty of his administration in a still-memorable farewell address. "We have, like the Arabs, only to 'fold our tents and silently steal away,' congratulating ourselves that this is the only 'stealing' which has been performed by this Honorable Body."

Bridgeport was extremely hospitable, and profitable, for the doctors Warner. Business was so good that within a year or two, the previously poor, struggling farm boys were both millionaires.

To be quite candid about this success, and after studying the drawings of ensuing products which followed the first corset-waist, an historian must draw the conclusion that many of the altruistic principles on which the business was founded (such as suspending weight from the shoulders and not compressing the waist) were sacrificed by the good doctors on the altar of fashion and financial exigency. Fashion decreed a small waist; women wanted a small waist; they bought corsets that would give them a small waist; the doctors Warner designed and made corsets that gave their customers a small waist. As early as the first year of the new business, Lucien was admitting that they had "lengthened the front of their product, making it more like the regular type of garment and making it more difficult to get an easy fit." From that time on their corsets, while incorporating many new ideas, did not differ materially from those of their competitors and probably were no healthier. By 1878 Lucien could report rather proudly that the average waist size of their corsets was

Fig Leaves and Fortunes

The Coraline corset was Warner's most profitable product in the 1870s and 1880s. Mary Anderson was the most popular actress of the day.

18, 19, or 20 inches, a waist span which few women indeed could achieve without severe corset discomfort. In fact, they designed a so-called "Century" corset-shield which, according to their own explanation, "eased the strain on the corset bones where they were bent inward at the waistline to accomodate the tightly laced waists."

And they had to follow the dictates of fashion. When Worth in Paris decreed the death of the crinoline and the birth of the bustle, the doctors Warner produced their own version of how to wear the bustle in the form of Taylor's Folding Bustle, an ingenious product with metal hoops which folded up when a lady sat down. When the lady stood up, the hoops conveniently fell back into place. Such devices, quite naturally, led to absurdities like the designer in London who invented a bustle containing a music box which played "God Save the Queen" every time the wearer sat down.

Their biggest money maker, however, was not a design, but a technological development, the "Coraline Corset." At that time corsets were generally boned with horn or whalebone, which tended to stiffen and break. The doctors heard of, and learned how to use, the fibre of the Mexican ixtile plant, called Tampico grass, which, when tempered, made an unbreakable, but still flexible, boning material. Lucien wrote, "The Coraline Corset was a great success from the start, and soon we had one entire building devoted to the hackling of this Tampico fiber, a large floor in the main factory devoted for machinery for winding the coraline, and the larger part of another floor fitted up with huge presses heated with steam, in which we inserted the sections of the corsets and pressed and tempered the

1874 - 1888

Faultless Fit and Graceful Figure. Four Million women are to-day wearing Dr. Warner's Coraline Corsets. **Are YOU?**
Warner Bros., makers, N. Y. & Chicago.

Fashionably dressed women were used to advertise Warner's corsets in the 1880s.

BLISSFUL DREAMS ASSURED BY USING WARNER BROS CORALINE CORSETS.

OVER.

Wild imagination was also used in some Warner's ads in the early days.

coraline." For ten years more than three-quarters of the firm's products were made with this coraline stiffening. An 1883 advertisement in *Harper's Bazaar* showed the "Four Most Popular Corsets in America" to be the Coraline Corset, the Coraline Health Corset, the Flexible Hip Corset, and the Coraline Abdominal Corset, all by the doctors Warner. Probably the success of coraline was best expressed by the unknown poet who wrote in her school newspaper,

> *Oh, sing me a song, mother dear,*
> *A song of the sweet Coraline,*
> *Ah, what is this word that I hear*
> *Alike from the milkmaid and queen?*
>
> *Why is she so shapely and sweet?*
> *Why is she so jolly and smart?*
> *Why is she so light on her feet?*
> *And always so light in her heart?*
>
> *Oh, sing me a song that will tell*
> *The magic that lies in this name,*
> *To make every maiden a belle,*
> *And beautify every old dame.*

Meanwhile, the wave of incoming immigrants was producing wretched slums. The city, said Lord Bryce in his *American Commonwealth*, was the one conspicuous failure of American democracy. In those cities population grew far faster than facilities to house the new

1874 - 1888

arrivals. The result was tenements, five and six-story high, firetraps, rickety, dirty, ill-ventilated, without plumbing or in many cases, heat. One block in the lower East Side of New York contained 2,781 inhabitants, but not a single bathtub.

The city of Bridgeport was no exception; there too the tenements were miserable. By 1886, only twelve years after its founding, Warner Brothers employed some 1,500 workers, nine-tenths of them women. These women, at first New England farm girls, then later immigrants from Hungary, Poland, Italy, and other European countries, lived in the slums of lower Bridgeport, in poverty and loneliness.

The doctors Warner, concerned with the living conditions of their workers, decided to help. DeVer explained, "Many of our girls live in abject poverty. They are obliged to spend a large proportion of their earnings for room and board. In some instances the food furnished at boarding houses is of an inferior quality and poorly cooked. Then there are some who are obliged to pass their evenings either on the street or alone in their rooms . . . they are deprived of the comforts of life." To make life more pleasant for these workers, and to give them something to do in the evening, the doctors Warner built a home-away-from-home opposite the factory, and called it the "Seaside Institute." It contained a restaurant, where meals were served at cost, a library and reading room, a music room, and two halls where classes were given in singing, penmanship, drawing, book-keeping, and fancy sewing. In addition it contained lavatories. The company boasted, "Great pains have been taken in fitting up an elegant toilet room which contains six bathtubs supplied with hot and cold water."

Mrs. Grover Cleveland, wife of the President, came from Washington for the dedication of the Seaside Institute on November 10, 1887. P.T. Barnum, who had given encouragement for the project, was there. So was a large gathering of prominent men and women who heard Dr. I.DeVer Warner say, "We have planned this Institute as a clubhouse for working women. In our imagination we have seen these rooms thronged night after night with happy, cheerful faces. We have seen the hand of toil made lighter, the burdens and cares of life easier, by reason of the rest and recreation obtained in these rooms." Mark Twain was invited, accepted, but then did not attend, blaming his wife who had accepted another invitation. He wrote to Mrs. Cleveland, "I do not know how it is in the White House, but in this house of ours whenever the minor half of the administration tries to run itself without the help of the major half, it gets aground. . . . The fact is I had forgotten that we were to have a dinner party on that Bridgeport date . . . the other end does not forget these things. . . . Just so with a funeral; if it is the man's funeral, he is most always there, of course, but that is no credit to him; he wouldn't be there if you depended on *him* to remember it. . . . Of course, I am not going to say anything against funerals — that is, as occasions — mere occasions — for as diversions I don't think they amount to much. But as I was saying — if you are not busy I will look back and see what it was that I was saying . . . I don't seem to find the place. But any way she was as sorry as anybody could be that I could not go to Bridgeport."

The construction of Seaside Institute, unique as it was in American industry, brought praise for the Warners from all sorts of people at home and abroad. *Century Magazine* went overboard. "In these days when the hearts of the compassionate are torn by so many harrowing tales of man's inhumanity to working-women it is pleasant to be able to set forth the good deeds of these two chivalrous employers. . . . If the women who work are to be rescued from their wretchedness, it must be done by such knightly employers as these who

Fig Leaves and Fortunes

decline to build their fortunes on the woes of women."

Unfortunately the praise for the Warners was not unanimous. Certain union organizations expressed their disapproval, and a writer in *The Workmen's Advocate* was very critical. "Dr. Warner, who is a stranger to me, may be a well-meaning philanthropist, but he certainly shows himself to be a poor doctor, for a good physician does not prescribe soothing syrup. . . . Why did Dr. Warner reduce the wages of his employees to such low rates as to make a cheap boarding house necessary for them? Let him show his practical philanthropy by first raising the wages of his help to living rates. . . . The working people want no charity. If justice was done to them, if they were not robbed of more than half the proceeds of their labor, there would be no need for cheap boarding houses."

Poster advertising Dr. Warner's Safe Nervine
found in a music hall in Skagway, Alaska.

4

1876 - 1925

WHILE THE POOR suffered in the slums, the last quarter of the nineteenth century was a time of glorious affluence for a few Americans. Those who had money flaunted it in lavish Victorian manner. They built ostentatious homes in a chaos of architectural styles, filled them with useless and ornate bric-a-brac, employed dozens of servants and gardeners, gave elaborate parties with the women dressed in the latest from Paris, and traveled world-wide in ultra first-class style. It was a great time to be alive, provided you were among the privileged.

Around 1876 the bustle disappeared, to be replaced by the train, often long and dragging in the street. John Ruskin wrote, "I have lost much of the faith I once had in the common sense and personal delicacy of fashionable women by seeing how they allow their dresses to sweep the streets, as if it is the fashion to be scavengers."

Rather quickly trains went out of fashion for daytime but were worn as a separate attachment for evening. The dress itself covered the body from neck to knee as tightly as possible, held in by a tight, heavily boned corset. Only below the knee did the dress flare out. In some extreme cases the knees were actually tied together so that the wearer could take only short, mincing steps, which was considered a very flattering way to walk.

But the bustle was not finished. It had a sharp revival in 1882 and within a year or two was seen again on almost all fashionable women. It was not until September 1888 that the Rational Dress Society's *Gazette* could announce with considerable relief that the bustle was finally gone. "Worth now eschews even the semblance of a bustle. We will now actually be able to lean back in a carriage or in a chair once more."

The once simple life-style of the doctors Warner had changed with the success of their company. They were now part of the business, social, and fashion elite. Dr. I. DeVer Warner's home near Seaside Park in Bridgeport and Dr. Lucien's home at Irvington-on-Hudson looked like baronial castles. In Bridgeport DeVer became an important figure in the community's business and social life. With his friend, P.T.Barnum, he organized the Citizens

Above, Dr. I. DeVer Warner's home near Seaside Park in Bridgeport circa 1885. Below, Dr. Warner's study.

1876 - 1925

The original Warner Hall at Oberlin College built in 1884 as a conservatory of music through the generosity of Dr. Lucien Warner.

Water Company, later consolidated with the Bridgeport Hydraulic Company, with himself as president. He was president of the Bridgeport Gas Company and a director of the New York, New Haven, and Hartford Railroad. If along with running the Warner Brothers Company, all this did not fill his time, he was a prominent member of the First Presbyterian Church and an organizer of the Brooklawn Country Club and of the Bridgeport Y.M.C.A., of which he was, of course, president.

The chief beneficiary of Lucien Warner's new wealth was Oberlin College. As early as December 30, 1882, he wrote President James Fairchild, "My wife and I have long had it in mind to do something for Oberlin, and it is fully one year ago that we began to consider the erection of a conservatory building for the Music School." At the dedication of Warner Hall December 20, 1884, the catalogue described it as "the finest building ever erected for the use of a school of music either in this country or, as far as we know, in Europe." President Fairchild praised Lucien Warner, "I have followed Dr. Warner's career with a delight that has increased with the increase of his prosperity. . . . Nor must I forget to pay tribute to her who today shares with him the joy of this dedication service. There is an old saying in Scotland that a man will be no richer than his wife will let him. It is just as true that a man will be no more generous than his wife will let him be."

Lucien was both humble and eloquent in his response. "I am glad to make this return to my alma mater which enabled me, a poor boy of eighteen, to come here with less than $100 in my pocket, and with this capital and my own labor to take a five-year course of

Fig Leaves and Fortunes

Warner Gymnasium, built in 1901, was also given to Oberlin by Dr. Warner. It is now a fine arts building.

study. It was with a spade on the land where the Ladies' Hall now stands that I first studied the principles of drainage. It was with a kit of carpenter's tools in repairing old Tappan Hall, Colonial Hall, and Ladies' Hall that I acquired my early lessons in building and architecture."

The second building given to Oberlin by Lucien and his wife was the Warner Gymnasium, completed in 1901. The original building for the conservatory has since been torn down, replaced in a different location by the Warner Concert Hall, a 1963 gift in Lucien's honor by his daughter and son-in-law. The gymnasium, however, still stands, now used as a fine arts building.

Regardless of their worldly success, the doctors Warner still restlessly pursued new ideas for making new money. In their corset business there were frequent new designs, now tied closely to the changing fashions. With bustles they were in and out, then in and out again. When the front of the dress became flat and tight, they made flat and tight corsets. They had their own representatives in Paris flashing news to them of the latest turns of the haute couture. For what Paris ordered, America and Warner Brothers obeyed. When Redfern, an Englishman in Paris, became the dean of the fashion world, Warner's made corsets designed in collaboration with him and sold under the Redfern name. In 1885 they began importing expensive garments made in England by a William Pretty, a famous corset designer of the time. These styles, dubbed W. B., were more expensive than American corsets and made in the French manner with one thickness of body material instead of two. Women liked them because they were lighter than the American models.

1876 - 1925

Ad for Dr. Warner's Health Underwear, which turned out to be a financial disaster.

But there were failures too. At one time they made baseballs in their Bridgeport plant, but the venture was quickly dropped. A more conspicuous failure was "Dr. Warner's Health Underwear," made of wool and camel's hair and advertised as protection against winter colds. Lucien Warner wrote, "We pushed the business vigorously for seven years, charging off a loss of from six to twenty thousand dollars each year, until finally in 1893 we closed out the business with a total loss of over one hundred thousand dollars." This was not to be the last time that Warner's would venture into the underwear business.

Dr. Lucien Warner, operating out of New York, appears to have been more susceptible to risky business ventures than his brother in Bridgeport who confined himself to what were then relatively secure community enterprises such as water and gas companies, banks, and railroads. Lucien confides that the first investment he ever made was the purchase of a farm near McGrawville, which he sold ten years later for half what he paid for it. After several loans to needy friends who never paid them back, he invested in a New York wallpaper business, which was soon written off as a complete loss. He then put money into an orange grove in Okahumpka, Florida, which was devastated by twin freezes in 1893. His next venture was a copper mine in Arizona. The young man who was the promoter of this speculation was, as Lucien Warner explains, "soon after a fugitive from justice, and although arrested once or twice, has managed to forfeit his bail and so escape punishment."

But the most ambitious personal investment which Lucien Warner made was in the Warner Chemical Co. He got into this through an interest in a deposit of phosphate of alumina on Grand Connetable Island, near what was then French Guiana. The problem was that there was very little use for the phosphate as it was not in soluble form. After many frustrating years marked by falsifications in accounting by a trusted bookkeeper and a disastrous fire, the company was still losing money and never did become profitable. Lucien observed, "This experience is but another illustration of the well-established principle that success in any line of endeavor is to be attained only by thorough preparation." Lucien himself seems to have had the habit of jumping into ventures without adequate preparation, contrary to his own advice.

Fortunately there was always the corset business churning out money.

Fig Leaves and Fortunes

Mrs. Eva Follett Warner, bride of Dr. I. DeVer Warner, in her wedding dress, 1896.

1876 - 1925

Gradually the brothers began to give up day-to-day responsibility for their businesses. DeVer owned a succession of sea-going yachts on which he leisurely and sumptuously cruised the New England coast in the summer and established a winter home in Augusta, Georgia. His wife, Lucetta, whom he had married back in McGrawville days, died in 1895, and he married Eva Follett, beautiful and twenty-six years of age, thirty-one years his junior. She had been born in Sheldonville, Massachusetts, the daughter of a poet and a New York banker. She grew up in New York and attended Miss Reed's exclusive private school and the famous Dodsworth Dancing Classes where she met John D. Rockefeller Jr. Through him, she met his illustrious father, John D. Sr., with whom she and her husband developed a life-long friendship. Probably it was no coincidence that the Rockefellers were neighbors in Augusta where DeVer and Eva spent the long winters at their home named "Magnolia Villa." There DeVer could enjoy the mild weather so different from the winters of his boyhood on the northern farm. It was there too that he died on January 11, 1913.

Ira Warner, the son of DeVer and Eva, wrote about the friendship between his mother and father and John D. "My father more or less retired in 1900 and built a house in Augusta, Georgia. Shortly thereafter Mr. Rockefeller began spending his winters at the Bon Air Hotel just a block from my father's house. Since my father and Mr. Rockefeller were the same age and both were golf enthusiasts, they played golf together almost every day, but never on Sunday. Nearly every Sunday after church Mr. and Mrs. Rockefeller would come to our house for dinner in the middle of the day.

"After my father's death my mother sold the Augusta house. The following year Mr. Rockefeller bought a home in Ormond Beach. He asked my mother to visit him there, which she did and continued to do from periods of two weeks to three months up until the time he died in May 1937. I often used to go with her to Ormond and also to his beautiful home at Pocantico Hills, near Tarrytown, New York. We took several motor trips with him lasting for a few days to two weeks. Such a trip consisted of a cavalcade of three cars. His, of course, then one for the secretary, valet, and maid, and the third was a station wagon loaded down with luggage.

"Whether at Ormond or Pocantico, breakfast was always at eight. Everyone came down (there were usually ten or twelve people at the table) and it was a formal meal of three or four courses. The head butler, Michael, stood behind Mr. Rockefeller and waited entirely on him. Each morning when Mr. Rockefeller came down, he would go straight to the kitchen, say, 'Good Morning,' to all the help (there were a lot of them) and give them each a dime. But he would never let any of them have an egg for breakfast. He had never had one as a boy, and he felt they were a luxury. Then he would come back into the dining room and give all his guests a dime. My mother had over a thousand dimes. After breakfast he would read out loud to his guests from a book he liked which he thought would be uplifting.

"Golf was on the Ormond Beach Golf Course only a few hundred yards from his home. There was always a crowd of winter tourists to see him tee off, and if there were any children, he would give them each a dime.

"Lunch was promptly at one-thirty, and about three o'clock Mr. Rockefeller would take a long drive in a car. He had two open Crane Simplex, so exactly alike that the chauffeur had painted #1 and #2 on the cylinder block of each car to tell them apart. If we were at Pocantico, we could drive for an hour without ever going off the thirty-three thousand acres of the estate with its thirty miles of paved roads.

Fig Leaves and Fortunes

Dr. I. DeVer Warner and John D. Rockefeller golfing in Augusta, Georgia in the early 1900s.

1876 - 1925

"Dinner was at seven-thirty. All the men wore dinner jackets, and no cocktails or wine were ever served, and no one smoked. One night Mr. Rockefeller's daughter, Mrs. Prentice, was at the table, having just returned from Europe. Before leaving, she had left some money with her father to invest, and now she wanted it back. When he came to the dinner table, he had a check in his pocket which he handed down the table to her. To her great joy the check was for considerably more than she had left with him. What the original amount was I never knew, but Mrs. Prentice showed me the check he had just given her, and it was for seventeen million dollars."

Such were the friendships Dr. I. DeVer Warner, the former farm boy, and his young, attractive wife came to enjoy. Like many of their compatriots, they lived in the grand style, if not quite like the Rockefellers, at least better than most Americans at the turn of the new century. In the memory of those who knew him or heard tales of him, DeVer Warner, at least in his prosperous old age, was noted as a stickler for efficiency, with little patience for incompetence, perhaps a difficult husband and taskmaster. His granddaughter tells of the time her grandmother Eva was entertaining friends for tea when DeVer arrived home. One of the ladies asked if she was sitting in his chair. He replied gruffly, "Madam, they are all my chairs." He resisted buying a car as long as possible, saying that a horse and buggy was much more reliable. When he finally did buy a car, he never learned to drive, but always had a chauffeur. He would usually retire to bed by eight or nine o'clock at night, maintaining that an hour's sleep before midnight was worth two hours afterwards. He was known on occasion to go upstairs to bed at nine o'clock even if there were guests present. Quite understandably, Eva, who loved a party, did not appreciate this.

In spite of his eccentricities, he was remembered with affection by many of his neighbors and employees. Joe Hurley, a neighbor who grew up in the South End of Bridgeport, wrote, "Kids in the South End at the turn of the century will always be grateful to DeVer Warner who lived in the big 'Red House' at Park Place and Myrtle Avenue for the July Sweets apple orchard in his big back yard, where, if Mike Solen, the caretaker, wasn't looking, you could get a shirt full of those luscious apples after a wind storm. It was 'Big Mike' who lavished the care and affection on those famous Warner gardens of flowers and who could be seen out early in the morning and into the evening, and still had time to raise a family at the live-in cottage on the Warner estate. Mike was still around when they tore down that 'Red House' mansion and cried unashamed tears as the wreckers ate into what was one of the finest houses ever built. It was there that Grover Cleveland came as a guest when he was President of the United States. It was a treat to see the beautiful ladies arrive in their horse-drawn carriages to attend a social function at the home of Dr. Warner. Those were the grand days!"

DeVer Warner's great-grandson, Stuart Warner, can also reminisce about those days in Seaside Park, Bridgeport, when, after Dr. Warner's death, he lived near "Aunt Eva's house," before it was torn down. "Mike, who once worked for P.T. Barnum, would let me ride the horse as we pulled a mower around the property, and he had many a tale to tell. Among them was the one about Barnum having a camel and an elephant hitched to Mike's mower at Barnum's place near the railroad tracks. This was to get publicity for the circus when the excursion trains went by.

"Well do I remember those early days. The clip-clop of the ice wagon horse coming down Lafayette Street, also the Warner factory whistle, so nearby, blowing early in the morn-

Fig Leaves and Fortunes

The pleasure of your company is requested on Friday evening, March 13th at eight o'clock at the residence of Dr. Lucien C. Warner, 2012 Fifth Avenue, for a conference upon the work and aims of the Charity Organization Society and the evils of indiscriminate alms giving.

The Hon. Grover Cleveland, will preside.

President Grover Cleveland and Lucien C. Warner were close friends.

ing and late in the day. Locomobiles were tested on Park Place — driven by mechanics sitting on wooden boxes, the bodies of the cars not having been installed yet."

Lucien Warner also began to withdraw from the corset business and became an eager traveler, making at least sixteen trips to Europe after his first excursion in 1880. He also went twice around the world and visited Egypt, Mexico, Puerto Rico and the Caribbean, Japan, China, India, Singapore, Australia, and New Zealand, plus innumerable trips around the United States. It was as if, having spent his youth in the confines of an isolated farm in upper New York state, he was determined to expand his horizons to the limit. These horizons even extended to his personal friendships which included five presidents of the United States. He first met President Rutherford Hayes at Oberlin and saw him frequently at various charity conferences. Mrs. Hayes in those days was known as "Lemonade Lucy" because she refused to serve alcoholic beverages at her parties. Lucien liked her, nevertheless, and commented, "She could discuss philosophy, politics, or talk the lightest nonsense with equal skill and fluency." President Grover Cleveland was probably Lucien's closest presidential friend and he and Karen were invited often to the White House. In addition he knew Presidents Harrison, Taft, and Theodore Roosevelt, of whom he wrote, "Mr. Roosevelt had a habit of assuming a very confidential manner with those with whom he conversed, and of saying many things that it would not be discreet to publish." Lucien, of course, was always discreet.

On April 12, 1918, Lucien and Karen celebrated their fiftieth wedding anniversary at a family luncheon attended by sixteen children and grandchildren, to each of whom they gave a present. This was followed by a second wedding journey to White Sulphur Springs. From there Lucien wrote, "The bride of this trip is the same, and yet not the same, as the one of fifty years ago. Something of the bloom and freshness of the cheeks is absent and the abundant auburn hair is now nearly white, but in their place there are lines which record growth in experience, wisdom, patience, sweetness and affection. Who shall say that the change is not for the better? Certainly not the bride-groom, whose own profusion of black hair is now white and none too abundant. The years have dealt kindly with him, but the daily record of half a century is plainly engraven on his face and his step has lost something of the spring and elasticity of youth. All of this is only a part of the process of nature in ripening her fruits. We believe with Browning:

'The best is yet to be,
The last of life for which the first was made.'"

Three years later, on his eightieth birthday, Lucien wrote to his family and friends: "Happiness is to be found only in service to our fellow-men. 'He that loseth his life for My sake, shall find it.' The conditions of human happiness may all be expressed in the one word — 'Love'— Love to God and Love to our fellow-men.

"I do not give this as the creed I have faithfully followed all my life. Alas, I have fallen far short of it, but I give it as the creed that my eighty years of observation and experience have clearly demonstrated is the only one that brings true happiness. As such, I pass it on as my birthday gift to all who might wish to share in my experience."

Dr. Lucien C. Warner died on July 30, 1925. He was eighty four.

5

1888 - 1914

W ALL STREET owns the country," thundered the woman revisionist, Mary Ellen Lease. "Our laws are the output of a system that clothes rascals in robes and honesty in rags." The Populist Presidential Platform of 1892 declared, "The fruits of the toil of millions are boldly stolen to build up colossal fortunes for a few. . . . From the prolific womb of governmental injustice we breed the two great classes, tramps and millionaires."

For the nation the period from about 1890 to World War I witnessed a dramatic clash between those in political, economic, and social authority, who liked things the way they were, and those on the outside, who saw in the country only corruption, injustice, poverty, slums, and "malefactors of great wealth." It was popular to be a reformist; men like William Jennings Bryan, Theodore Roosevelt, and Robert LaFollette knew that. They were the leaders in the Age of Reform.

But the bastions of entrenched power and wealth were not easily torn down. For those who had created wealth for themselves, like the doctors Warner, had also created wealth, even if unevenly distributed, for others and for the nation. In so doing, they, the businessmen, popular or not, had become the most important figures in the everyday life of both the great cities of America and the smaller communities like Bridgeport, Connecticut. This was an astonishing change from the days immediately after the Civil War when the doctors Warner had considered taking up careers in law, education, medicine, or the ministry as the only respectable occupations for ambitious young men. At the turn of the century wealthy businessmen, in spite of the efforts of the reformers, still controlled the lives of millions of workers, paid no income taxes, and were subject to little or no governmental regulations. Nationally there were men like the merchants, John Wanamaker of Philadelphia and Marshall Field of Chicago, ranchers like the King family of Texas, lumbermen like Frederick Weyerhaeuser, railroaders like James J. Hill and Edward H. Harriman, meat packers like the Armours and Swifts, tobacconists like James B. Duke, and perhaps most importantly of all, because he changed the way of life of all Americans, Henry Ford.

In the world of Bridgeport, Connecticut, there was also such a man. He was D.H. Warner, the son of Dr. I. DeVer Warner. "D.H.", as he was always called, had come to work for his father's firm in 1887, and beginning in 1894, when the company was legally changed from a partnership to a corporation, he dominated Warner Brothers, the corset industry, and to a great extent the city of Bridgeport for a period of forty years. In addition to being president of Warner's, he ran the Bridgeport Hydraulic Company, the Bridgeport Gas Light Company, and the mercantile business of the area's largest department store, D.M. Read's. He was a director of the Bridgeport National Bank, president of the Mountain Grove Cemetery Association, and a vice-president of the Bridgeport Hospital. He was an advisor to a succession of Bridgeport mayors, ran several campaigns for state and local Republican political candidates, and had close associations with the city's trolleycar company and the New York, New Haven, and Hartford Railroad. If you lived in Bridgeport, in the surrounding towns, or, in fact, anywhere in the state of Connecticut, he was a man to be reckoned with.

Yet he had but little education. He was born when his parents still lived in McGrawville and moved with them to Bridgeport when he was eight. There he went to private schools and was taught by a tutor. At nineteen he went into his father's corset company with no more formal learning. But he did absorb the details of the business, serving an apprenticeship in every department, until he was a master of them all. His business letters show the scope of his knowledge and his concern with detail, not only in the corset trade but also in the other enterprises he organized and ran. A big man, six feet tall and well over 200 pounds, he was equally as absorbed in play as in work. An amateur boxer in his youth, he once went four rounds with heavyweight champion, Bob Fitzsimmons. He was a baseball player, a racing sailor and yachtsman, a golfer, a flute player, and one of the pioneer automobilists in the area. He owned the first of the high-powered, chain-driven, bucket seat, automobiles produced by the made-in-Bridgeport Locomobile Company. He dressed carefully and well, loved good times, good food, good liquor and good wines, good cigars, and good company. All this made him a lively companion in the early, good years, but eventually contributed to the debility of his old age.

In the women's fashion world a controversy existed too — between the traditionalists and the reformists, and the corset, as usual, was at the center of the argument. Dresses in the late Victorian and early Edwardian years were notable for their ultra lavishness in yards of material and in adornment. The English fashion magazine, *The Lady*, observed in 1902, "Not only are the fabrics of exquisite texture, but they are embellished with miraculously fine hand embroidery, applique lace insertions and trimming of many kinds. Garnitures of pearls and groups of tinsel butterflies or dragonflies edged with garnitures of pearls or coral beads are favorite adornments." Beneath all the decorated yardage the corset remained firm and unmovable, anchored as always at the waist.

In the midst of this elaborate Edwardian dowdiness there suddenly appeared the Kangaroo Figure, made immortal in 1911 by the drawings of the American artist, Charles Dana Gibson. The dress of the Gibson Girl was long, straight, tight, and clinging, often with bare shoulders. Her busts protruded impressively, while her posterior thrust out like a bustle. For several years she caused millions of American women to desire a front as straight as a ruler and a back as curved as a camel's hump. No woman, no matter how slim, could achieve such a figure without the help of a firmly boned, tight, straight corset.

Perhaps it was the Gibson Girl, perhaps it was just common sense, but it was at about

Fig Leaves and Fortunes

In the early 1900s D.H. Warner produced rust-proof boning to replace buffalo horn and whalebone in moderately priced corsets.

1888 - 1914

this time that the reformists began to make *their* influence felt. They began experiment- ing with full, shapeless dresses worn without a corset. A few women followed their lead, but like their compatriots in the political and economic sphere, the reformists encountered difficulty selling their ideas. The appeal was, of course, that their dresses were healthy, that "the wearer of such a dress keeps the body fit for the functions of motherhood." One unconvinced traditionalist observed tartly, "As long as you wear that dress, you are hard- ly likely to get in that condition."

The doctors Warner must have experienced a feeling of deja vu if they read a widely distributed article written by a Berlin architect, Professor Schultze-Naumberg, in 1898. "The first thing to be considered is, of course, the corset—that female armour which is a threat to health, constricting chest and waist and endangering lungs, liver, and heart. The principle underlying the design of both outer and underclothes should be to transfer the center of gravity from waists and hips to the shoulders, which would seem to be the natu- ral weight bearers."

How similar to their own beliefs before the days of commercial success!

Certainly the last years of the old century and the first of the new, when D.H. was making his presence felt in the company and the community, were good years for Warner's. In its January session of 1893 the General Assembly of Connecticut passed a resolution incor- porating the Warner Brothers Company, "for the purpose of manufacturing, importing, buying, selling, and dealing in all kinds of corsets and wearing apparel." Sales the first year after incorporation were $1,856,600. By 1913 they were $7,005,786 with average yearly profits over $700,000 proving rather conclusively the outstanding leadership of D.H. Warner.

While D.H. was a man of enormous energy and wide-spreading community interests, he did, at least in the early years, give major attention to the corset business, on which his wealth depended. His first conspicuous achievement was "Rust-Proof" steel boning, des- tined to be the universal boning for the industry. Up to this time horn boning, made from East Indian buffalo horns, had been the standard stiffening material for inexpensive cor- sets, while whalebone was used for luxury articles. D.H. worked with a steel-wire company to produce the first completely rust-proof coated flat spring steel, which almost immedi- ately took the place of horn boning. It required some ten years, however, for Rust-Proof to displace whalebone in garments like Warner's Redfern line, the company's highest-priced product. Women who bought expensive corsets preferred whalebone, but whalebone was a commodity of varying quality and speculative price. The company had been in the prac- tice of buying whalebone slabs eight to fifteen feet long directly from Bering Sea whalers when the fleet returned from its three year voyage. More than half of the whalebone cut in America was cut by Warner's. They used the "shell," the surface layers, which was the top quality, for their corsets, and sold the rest for less demanding uses like boning dress- es. When Warner's finally abandoned whalebone in 1912, to adopt clock spring steel co- vered with hard rubber or celluloid, the move was delayed several months to permit the whaling fleet to return to port and sell its catch. The announcement of the change cut the whalebone price in half and, along with the refining of oil, helped end the sailing days of the romantic whaling ships of New Bedford and Nantucket.

Another early success for D.H. was the development of a corset which could also act as a hose supporter. Up to that time, hose supporters had been separate items fastened in

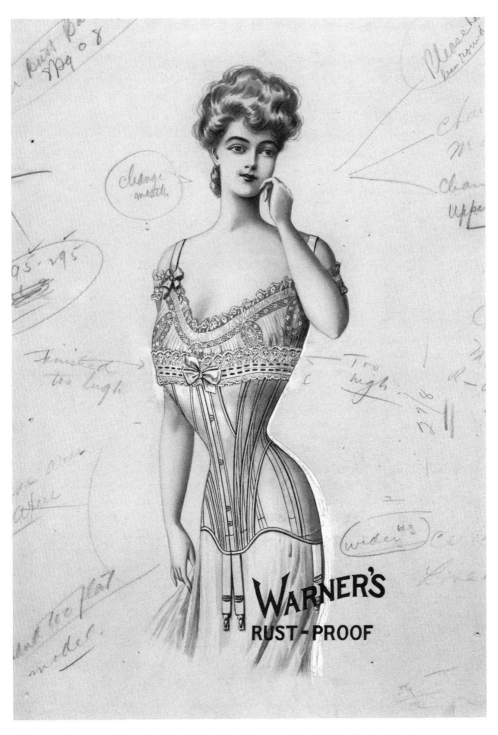

Illustration for a 1907 Warner's ad for its Rust-Proof line complete with the client's critique.

1888 - 1914

In 1901, one magazine rejected the ad at the left as indecent, and gratuitously added a chemise (right).

various ways to the waist. D.H. lowered the front of the corset and then extended the side down past the curve of the hip. The result was an entirely new-looking corset to which hose supporters could be directly attached. It also had the beneficial effect of anchoring the corset down on the hips, instead of only at the waist.

As the top of the corset dropped lower, the customary loose fitting "corset cover" no longer had a corset to cover. And so the brassiere appeared. There is controversy over who invented it. Industry researchers believe that it was a Charles R. DeBevoise in Paris in 1902 who named and pioneered it. His first brassiere was really a formfitting corset cover, long, with built-up shoulders, and was advertised for stout women. A more romantic version bestows the creation, at least of the short, minimum bra, on a certain Mary Phelps Jacob, later better known as Caresse Crosby, a glittering, almost fictional, American heiress. She got the idea when she was a New York debutante. In her book, *The Passionate Years*, she describes how she rebelled against wearing a corset, and how she and her maid one night before a dance made a bra from two pocket handkerchiefs, some pink ribbon, and thread. When friends liked it and asked her to make bras for them, she decided to patent her invention and exploit it. The patent was issued in 1915 and shortly thereafter, as the story goes, she sold it to Warner's for fifteen thousand dollars.

In the decade before World War I Warner's sales went booming upward, far beyond

Fig Leaves and Fortunes

Mamma won't care!
Water
can't hurt
her Corset!

WARNER'S RUST-PROOF

Warner's advertising in the early 1900s was provocative and popular.

the dreams of the old doctors Warner. Additions, almost yearly, were made to the Bridgeport plant. The company's products and their quality were uniformly good; their adherence to the dictates of fashion, absolute. But another weapon, just becoming a part of American selling techniques, was also responsible for the company's growth. This was advertising, in which Warner's was one of the nation's leaders. Another Warner was responsible for this. L.T. Warner (he was always called "L.T."), the son of Dr. Lucien, was an educated man. Born in New York City, he attended private schools there and spent two winters in Switzerland studying French and German. He followed his father to Oberlin, where, like his father, he served for many years as a trustee. After college he took a law degree at Columbia University in New York, and then, in 1901, moved to Bridgeport and went to work for Warner's, first in the advertising department, later adding export and sales supervision.

L.T. was a far different man from D.H., who was heavyset (in his old age, fat), a smoker and drinker, a convivial joiner, uninterested in religion or things intellectual, a born promotor and leader, positive in his opinions, intolerant of the opinions of others. L.T., on the other hand, was frail, literate, rather austere, an abstainer, deeply religious, and sincerely interested in the opinions of others. D.H.'s energies were concentrated on business and pleasure. L.T. was not as good a business man, his energies turned toward music, art, books, and to church and charities. What he could contribute to the Warner company was a creative talent and a sense of humor, both of which are reflected in the unusual

It even tried to persuade women to wear the
Rust-Proof line in the summer and in
swimming.

advertising of his day, produced under his inspiration and direction. Redfern and Warner's were promoted in full color illustrations on gowned figures by well-known artists like Hanatschek, Popini, and Mucha. He started a series of letters to retailers from Warner's own fashion representative in Paris; he signed up the dancer, Mrs. Vernon Castle, for a testimonial ("The Redfern Corset is really more comfortable than none at all."); he opened corset schools for retail salesgirls; he placed the largest electric signs in the world, flashing "Warner's" over New York's Broadway and Chicago's Michigan Avenue; and he produced a motion picture featuring two children, a dog, a fountain, and a Warner's corset, which was distributed through the new medium of the moving picture houses.

L.T.'s daring reached a sort of climax in 1914. That was the year of the appearance of the "Natural Figure." L.T. explained: "Corsets had been illustrated in advertising as though worn over voluminous petticoats. We felt that the corset should be shown actually as it *was* worn. Ads were created showing the legs below the corset in pen and ink drawings by the artist Popini." The *Boston Transcript* and *Vogue* magazine refused to run them because they thought they were indecent, but many other newspapers and magazines did run them. The ads caused Franklin P. Adams, writing in the *New York Tribune's* "The Conning Tower," to compose the following:

> "To The Redfern Corset Lady
> Lady, I was never one to flatter,
> Never one to pull the insincere
> Ever am I chary with my chatter;
> Few the frails for whom I fill an ear.
> Diffidness and shyness are my habit;
> Frightened as any forest fawn;
> Timid I as any startled rabbit;
> Shrinking as Orion at the dawn.
> Yet I feel no trace of any shyness,
> Hurling elegiacs at your head,
> Speaking of your obvious divineness—
> Not a fear, anxiety, or dread.
> Cast the gyve and break the galling fetter!
> Far away discretion's chain I throw,
> Lady, for I feel I know you better
> Than most any other girl I know."

Fig Leaves and Fortunes

Corset fitters were often featured in Warnaco ads. This was about 1910.

1888 - 1914

L.T. Warner often used gowned figures to advertise Warner's corsets. These elegant ladies of 1914 promoted the Redfern line.

Reformists of the times, noting the injustice of man to man, directed their ire particularly at the nation's garment factories. There children as young as five or six worked as day laborers. In these sweatshops, with their poor lighting and ventilation, wages were as low as three dollars a week. At the piece rates paid, workers rarely made more than $200 a year, taking into account the amount of time they were laid off. The Populist Party, the Socialists, the Progressives, and finally Theodore Roosevelt all took their turn in trying to do something about the situation, but their efforts were largely ineffectual.

Conditions at the Warner's plant in Bridgeport were better than that, but certainly not ideal. For his time D.H. Warner was actually an enlightened employer. He had the example before him of his father's and uncle's generosity to their workers in the creation of the Seaside Institute. It is true that he thought of himself first, his workers only second, but contrary to many employers of his time he *did* think of the workers. For instance, he was responsible for persuading his father, during the blizzard of 1888, to comfortably house and feed in the Seaside Institute those employees who for several days were unable to get home because of the snow. And the fact that he was very conscious of the reformist movement and its implications for employers like himself is proved by a remarkable letter written in 1911 to a woman who had questioned him about working conditions in his factory. He explained that Warner's employed close to 4,000 workers, 80 percent of whom were women. Hours of work were ten hours a day from Monday through Friday and five hours on Saturday, a total of 55 hours. Earnings in the sewing rooms varied from $7.36 per week to $12.81, with average take-home pay of $9.00. Ventilation was watched "as closely as

Fig Leaves and Fortunes

possible." The sanitary arrangements were "complete"; there were inspectors who went through the plant every day to check on cleanliness; there was an organized hospital corps with a doctor plus one or two trained nurses, who were prepared to treat any employee at any time for both major and minor ailments. If an employee was incapacitated by an accident, he or she was given a percentage of earnings while not able to work. He added, "My own judgment is that employers should assume the general responsibility for their people; pay them well; treat them well; help the unfortunate. My life has been spent with working people. I have tried conscientiously to cooperate with them, feeling that their prosperity and mine are one and the same. I believe that no form of labor should be allowed under sixteen years of age; that no laborer at sixteen should be allowed to work without a certification of education and a certificate of health."

D. H. sounded in this letter as if he were writing a tract for the reformist movement.

He was also very personally involved in the lives of his associates. Witness the letter he wrote in 1910 to the son of Charles Abbott, head of New York Sales, at the time of Mr. Abbott's serious illness. "I don't believe you thoroughly realize your father's condition. I have been watching him pretty closely and he surely is in bad shape. My own judgment is that he should at once take a rest. If Dr. Endicott could say to him that he had better slow up a while, then he would naturally come to me and ask for his vacation. This would be arranged."

And D.H. could be generous to men and women not in his employ. In March of 1910 he wrote to the Bridgeport Superintendant of Police. "I am informed that Policeman Deitz, recently killed while on duty, was not a member of the Police Association; consequently those dependent upon him would not be entitled to the usual benefits. Will you kindly see that the enclosed check is forwarded to his family?"

But D. H. was not generous to the point of sacrificing any of his own interests. He was a shrewd Yankee trader, determining early that he would work for no enterprise in which he did not have a substantial ownership and a chance to make money, and a lot of it, if the enterprise succeeded. He had a large stake in Warner Brothers, which was augmented by regular receipts of new preferred stock. In addition he had an incentive contract, one of the first in American business. At a special meeting of the board on May 11, 1908, his salary was raised to $30,000 per year plus 10 percent of company earnings in excess of $300,000 per year. At the same time he was a manager of the Bridgeport Hydraulic Co. and the Bridgeport Gas Light Co. Dissatisfied with his financial arrangement with the latter, he wrote in 1904 to ask for the right to buy company stock at a discount. "I am desirous of getting some returns for my labor. If I am going on to assist in developing the gas interests in the City of Bridgeport, I want to feel justified in giving it sufficient time. If I could make my holdings an amount that would realize to me a substantial return, it would be my intention to take hold of the matter more seriously."

It is perhaps in his letters that D.H. most completely reveals his complex personality. Here was a man of incredible energy, a vast store of interests, superb in major business matters but equally at home in the utmost trivia; a man who loved to bargain, yet could spend money recklessly on luxuries, a vain man who gradually let himself go physically, a man of strong friendships and strong dislikes.

May 19, 1902, to a Mr. Struse. "About six weeks ago I ordered from H.D. Crippen, 52 Broadway, one of the 'Professional Punching Bags' with view of reducing my weight. Don't know whether he has not got them or whether he is afraid of my credit, but as my weight

Warner's most expensive product was the Redfern line, named after the famous couturier. This 1910 ad was one of the last to feature whalebone.

Fig Leaves and Fortunes

is increasing quite rapidly I am anxious to get it."

July 7, 1905, to Survey Map Co. "I received your letter refusing to accept return of maps which we found did not answer our purpose. . . . I want you to understand that I consider your business methods barbarous."

June 22, 1907, to Scandinavian Fur Co. "I am returning again today my cap you made for me. You first made it at 7 5/8 and it was so large I could not wear it. Now it is too small. I have been trying to stretch it with a hat stretcher, but I cannot keep it on my head."

November 30, 1907, to Mr. MacDonald. "I am sending in tonight's case my flute. It needs general overhauling."

May 7, 1909, to Dunlap & Co. "I want to buy a Panama hat, size 7¼ to cost not to exceed $25.00, prefer something a little less. I am six feet high and weigh a little over 200, although I don't like hats styled for big men."

May 13, 1909, to Dunlap & Co. "I am a bigger man than I thought. I must have a bigger hat."

July 7, 1909, to Wooster-Atkinson Co. "In reference to the enclosed bill, would say that according to my chauffeur the item of soap — 25 cents, should not be charged to me. Please return corrected bill."

November 2, 1910, to Dunlap & Co. "Will you send me one silk hat and one opera hat, size 7¼ in the latest style? I weigh 200 pounds, heavy rather than fat."

It was in the fall of 1902 that D.H. Warner bought his first automobile and became an immediate enthusiast. In the spring of that year he was still inquiring about single seat, horse-drawn carriages, a "good business wagon of respectable appearance." By November, however, we find him writing M.V. Doud of Bridgeport's Locomobile Co. to ask him to enter his order for a "Riker Gasolene Machine," being very specific as to what he wanted in the way of batteries, painting, length and width of the tonneau ("I see no reason why there should not be sufficient strength to carry a large, comfortable body."), upholstery, and even "tufted cushions." Other letters on his various automobiles:

April 16, 1906, to Winton Motor Carriage Co. "You state you can increase the speed of my model K runabout by giving me a higher gear. I wish you would ship me a higher gear. The car is used by my son, a boy seventeen years old. He has made some remarkable runs for a youngster but he can use a little more speed."

Jan 1, 1907, to Wm. W. Ogden. "I have smashed up the rear fender on the left-hand side of my Panhard car."

March 11, 1907, to Tichenor-Grand Co. "I am closing out my stable—going into automobiles. I have three horses, four sets of harness, four carriages, saddles, and some miscellaneous items to dispose of."

April 18, 1907, Tichenor-Grand Co. to D.H. Warner. "We regret exceedingly that you are disappointed with the sale but the market this spring has become suddenly flooded with second hand carriages, harness, etc., more than ever before in the history of the trade. This we presume is in consequence of so many people going in for automobiles."

March 27, 1907, Tichenor-Grand Co. to D.H. Warner. "We regret to say that a brewery wagon ran into your basket phaeton."

May 29, 1909, to Connecticut Railway and Lighting Co. "About ten days ago one of my chauffeurs demolished one of your trolley poles near the Brooklawn Club. The fault was entirely the man's, not the pole's."

One thing is certain. To have been D.H.'s son must have been a demanding assignment.

1888 - 1914

A Panhard & Levassor, one of D.H. Warner's early automobiles, circa 1908.

He was not one to tolerate weakness, at least in others. Sometimes his oldest boy, DeVer C. Warner (called "D.C.") did not live up to his expectations, and when that happened, the father's criticism could be biting. On January 31, 1911, we find D.H. writing young De-Ver, a Junior at Yale, who had overspent his allowance. "I won't waste much time going over the history of your finances. . . . I have tried to give you a liberal allowance, to have you realize that you are a dependent with no earning power, that you live through my generosity, that you should keep within your allowance. Up to date, you have not done so.

"I am a man of means. A certain portion of my fortune, you are entitled to. If you pro-pose to support your family and in my old age to help me and let me lean on you as my father has on me, you will have to curb your selfishness, organize yourself, and turn man."

There is no evidence of how D.C. responded to his father, but we do know that in late summer D.H. decided to discipline his son by forcing him to withdraw from college just at the beginning of Senior year and go to work. Dean Frederick S. Jones at Yale objected, pleading the boy's case, saying he had done well in college and deserved a chance to fin-ish. D.H. relented, agreed to let DeVer continue, and wrote Dean Jones. "I am a commer-cial, self-made man. I have worked hard for a great many years. Possibly some of the finer points of life do not appeal to me as much as to a man who has had less of hard work, hard knocks . . . and trouble. I have placed in the young man's hands real estate and secu-rities to an extent that give him an independent income. I also built and presented to him a home. This, in my judgement, has given the boy a somewhat wrong idea of the serious side of life. The young man some day will be the possessor of a third of my father's for-tune and mine. With it will come, if he has the ability, the control of the destinies of a great many thousands of people. Our combined interests today support in the neighbor-hood of 10,000 people. . . . I hope the boy will finish his college career with honors and that the future may prove my decision to let him continue is correct."

Fig Leaves and Fortunes

Alas, D.H.'s fortune was to be lost. Not by young DeVer, or by D.H.'s other children, Margaret or Bradford. It would be lost by D.H. himself.

Among the other activities on which D.H. kept a wary eye were those of the suffragettes, who under the efforts of feminists like Susan B. Anthony and Jane Addams were demanding equal rights with men and especially the right to vote. He was therefore somewhat concerned with the activities in 1910 of his own sister, Annie Bishop, married to the president of the New York, New Haven, and Hartford Railroad, who joined the suffragettes and started playing a leading role in a local chapter. Concerned about the reaction of her brother and father, Annie wrote to D.H. "It looks as though you and Father thought I had lost my head, my loyalty to family interests, and you feared I would lose my dignity in my interest in the suffrage question. Fear not; you know this subject is not to be seriously reckoned with for some years. It interests me, seems reasonable, and I feel is just, though I know the very forcible arguments against it from a manufacturer's point of view."

To this D. H. replied, "Don't let the suffrage movement worry you for a moment. I have never taken the matter seriously. It is a perfectly harmless form of amusement for any of you girls who want to take it up as a fad. If it should ever be taken seriously, we should fight it tooth and nail as we think it is about the worst form of socialism that could exist, but as long as it is so utterly harmless and faddish as organized at the present time it is to us nothing more than a subject of jest and ridicule."

Little did D. H. know how wrong he was. The Women's Suffrage Amendment, giving women the right to vote, was passed by Congress in 1917 and ratified by the necessary 36th state in 1919.

D.H. Warner was "Mr. Bridgeport." His correspondence just before World War I is evidence of his pervasive influence. We find him writing the Governor of Connecticut with advice, telling the Bridgeport Police Commissioner how to control the new problem of automobile traffic, suggesting routes for the city's trolley cars, complaining about the separate licenses required for driving in New York, New Jersey, and Connecticut, ordering the laying of new pipe for the Hydraulic Company, or, as a member of the board of Parks Commissioners proposing concerts for "the great mass of working people" in Beardsley and Seaside parks. He also ran the election campaigns for several Republican mayors, especially that of Clifford B. Wilson in 1911, who was running as a progressive reformer against the Democratic machine. Evidence of the bitterness he encountered in politics can be found in a letter to him from a lawyer friend, Charles S. Canfield, written just after the votes were counted. "I wish to congratulate you upon the result of the election, particularly in view of the dirty, mudslinging attacks made upon you through the columns of the *Farmer*."

D.H. was not one to tolerate mudslinging, certainly not against himself. To his employees at Warner Brothers he wrote, "It will be well for you to make it a rule to have no business dealings with the *Bridgeport Farmer*, either in advertising, special subscriptions, special editions or otherwise." At Warner's the rule of D.H. was absolute. There were no further dealings with the *Farmer*.

In spite of all his outside activity, D.H. was a daily, familiar figure to the thousands of Warner's employees who now occupied over 400,000 sq.ft. of factory space and constituted the largest and most important corset manufacturer in the world. When the salesmen met for their periodic sales conferences, D.H. was always the principal speaker and the center of attention. Typical of the sales conferences of those halcyon days was the an-

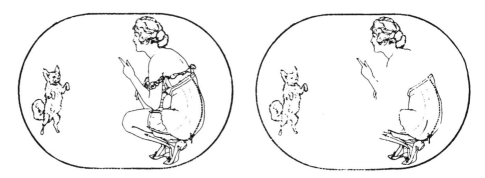

In 1914 the left illustration for a Warner ad was rejected by Vogue. *The retouched version passed the censor.*

nual convention in Bridgeport on December 19 and 20, 1912. Sales and profits were at an all-time peak, prospects for the year ahead good. The salesmen listened to the goals set out for them for 1913 (achieve a 20 percent increase in sales, feature the Redfern line, push accessories, sell every customer on every territory), then adjourned to Lehmann's Shore House for dinner (menu: Bronx cocktails, oysters on the half-shell, clam chowder, steamed clams, broiled mackerel, broiled chicken, boiled live lobster, french fried potatoes, crackers, cheese, and coffee. All this accompanied by Piels, Budweiser, Naugatuck, and Hydraulic beer). And they left the meeting with the words of the company theme song ringing in their ears.

> "Our Big Chief
> Our D.H., our D.H.
> Him big chief, eat em all alive.
> Big injin of the corset tribe,
> Some busy Iz, you bet he is.
> Swamp em, swamp em, get em wampum.
> Get the biz."

On a more sober, but still optimistic note, D.H. himself sat down to write his father on New Year's Eve. He reported on his many accomplishments during 1912 for the Warner Brothers Company, the Hydraulic Company, the Gas Company, and for the City of Bridgeport. In the latter case the new administration, which he had helped to get elected, had already "cleaned house" and lowered taxes. He was proud of his part in all this and wanted his father to know how well things were going and how hopeful the future looked.

He wrote just in time, because two weeks later his father was dead.

Fig Leaves and Fortunes

6

The Twenties

N SPITE OF the rough talk of the Progressives and the Revisionists, the period before World War I was a tranquil one. Of it, Walter Lipmann could write, "It was a happy time . . . the air was soft and it was easy to believe in the inevitability of progress, in the perfectability of man and of society, and in the sublimation of evil."

The war altered all that. It ushered in a period of change more rapid and confusing than any other in world history, a period continuing right up to the present. In the turbulent twenties, a decade that began in hope, was lived in confidence, and ended in disillusionment, the headlines in the morning papers told of civil war in Russia, of Woodrow Wilson's losing struggle to bring the United States into the League of Nations, the election of Warren Harding and the scandals that followed, the Red Scare raids and deportations. Remember Teapot Dome, Sacco-Vanzetti, Mah-Jongg, Coolidge prosperity, the Charleston, bathtub gin, Jack Dempsey, Babe Ruth, Rudolph Valentino? Prohibition, far from ending liquor, brought speakeasies, bootleggers, and gangsters. Scott Fitzgerald wrote, "The parties were bigger — the pace was faster — the shows were broader — the buildings were higher — the morals were looser — and the liquor was cheaper."

And it all ended in the Crash.

Women's fashions changed just as fast as history and fully reflected what was happening in life styles, manners, and morals. The fashion revisionists, long lamenting the evils of tight waists, boned bodices, and distended posteriors, finally had their day. The corset, as it had been known, disappeared.

It started during the war when millions of women, taking the place of men gone soldiering, went to work in the nation's offices and factories. There the cumbersome fashions of yesterday could not be worn. Simpler, cheaper, clothes were necessary. It continued in the twenties as women wore fewer clothes, especially undergarments. For the first time dresses crept above the knees, hair was bobbed, bathing suits were one piece and revealing. Instead of curves, the ideal figure became straight and masculine, minimizing the bust

51

During World War I hundreds of employees were transported to and from Warner's Bridgeport plant by this fleet of cars.

and the hips. As the *Pictorial Encyclopedia of Fashion* reported, "The dress became a tube, wider or narrower as required, with a larger opening for the legs, and a smaller one for the head, as well as two smaller tubes for the arms. . . . The female ideal of fashion had become an unusual creature, a hybrid of boy and girl, long-legged, flat-chested, with narrow hips and rather broader shoulders, and an Eton cap." From the middle of the twenties adventurous women even began to wear pants, a fashion which enabled them to actually look like men. As the old-fasioned corset disappeared, its place was taken by the elastic foundation garment, the girdle. Worn with a brassiere, together they simply flattened the hips and the chest.

All these changes had a dramatic effect on the corset industry, sharply reducing sales. Not only were fewer garments sold, but those that *were* sold were simpler, less expensive, and hence, less profitable. The good times were not going to roll forever for Warner's, or for D.H. Warner himself.

Things did go pretty well during World War I. Sales rose from $6,586,858 in 1912 to $12,651,448 in 1920; profits hit a peak of $1,593,311 in 1919. D.H. Warner, meanwhile, was earning $60,000 a year plus 10 percent of net profits over $600,000. "Net profit," in his case, was defined as "earnings exclusive of depreciation, pensions, income taxes, and other charges which the directors consider a charge against surplus rather than an expense of doing business." Inasmuch as D.H. controlled the board of directors he could decide himself what expenses should go in what accounts. His 1920 salary and bonus of over $175,000, determined by his own calculations, was an enormous sum in those days. In 1922 the board paid him additional compensation of $85,000 for undefined "extraordinary services." This payment was made from surplus.

Fig Leaves and Fortunes

The elaborate bungalow built by D.H. Warner in 1910 on Greenfield Hill in Fairfield.

All this income, however, began to slip through D.H.'s hands. He was already spending more money than he was earning. His yachts, his automobiles, his homes, his servants were all substantial costs. And he was adding to those costs. By 1910 he was building a summer place on Greenfield Hill, some ten miles from his home near the Warner's factory in Bridgeport. He wrote, "After twenty-five years of uninterrupted work I am indulging in my first plans for recreation in the building of a bungalow on Greenfield Hill. I hope to get the quiet and rest there that I am not able to get in the city." Some "bungalow!" In his recent history of Fairfield Thomas J. Farnam comments, "The town's wealthy residents continued to provide excitement. Greenfield Hill people followed the construction of De-Ver H. Warner's new summer residence with great interest. Who could ever have guessed there was so much money in corsets?"

In 1914 D.H. went farther by buying the Burr mansion, certainly the most historic house in Fairfield, perhaps in all the county. Originally built around 1700 by one Peter Burr, chief justice of the colony, it was owned during the Revolution by his grandson, Thaddeus, high sheriff of the county and close friend of the John Hancock family of Boston. It was to the Burr home in Fairfield that John Hancock and Samuel Adams fled in April 1775 after the Battle of Lexington, when the British had put bounties on their heads. They were accompanied by John's Aunt Lydia and his fiancée, the beautiful, flirtatious, Dorothy Quincy, who stayed in the Burr home while the men pushed on to the Continental Congress in Philadelphia. It was in the Burr home that John Hancock almost lost his bride to the dashing law student, Aaron Burr, cousin of Thaddeus, who lay seige to Dorothy, but was repulsed by the aunt.

And it was in the Burr homestead where John Hancock and Dorothy Quincy were mar-

The Twenties

The historic Burr mansion in Fairfield bought by D.H. Warner in 1914.

ried on August 28th, 1775. An historian commented on the "elegance and brilliancy of the toilets displayed by both men and women. Silver buckles, white silk stockings, knee breeches of varied hues, scarlet vests and velvet coats with ruffled shirts and broad fine neckware adorned the masculine fraternity, while the ladies were radiant in silks and laces, lofty head-dress, resplendent jewelry and the precious heirlooms of old families."

During the Revolution, George Washington, Benjamin Franklin, Lafayette, and John Adams were all vistors at the Burr mansion. So were Dr. Timothy Dwight, future president of Yale, and the artists Trumbull and Copley. But disaster struck in July 1779 when the British burned Fairfield, and with it, the Burr home, in spite of the promise of the British Commander, Governor Tryon, a frequent visitor to the house, to save it. A dramatic account of the ravagement of Mrs. Burr during the burning is given by Frank S. Child in his 1915 history of the Burr homestead. "The miscreants seized Mrs. Burr and stripped the silver buckles from her shoes. Others chased the frightened mistress through her house, attempting to despoil her of the very clothes she wore, throwing her down upon the ground . . . in their efforts to wrench from her grip a watch which she prized highly as a precious heirloom. They stole her pocket-book, snatched the gold sleeve buttons from her wrists, and drove her with frightened, struggling attendants into the meadow and thicket beyond the garden, where in the shelter of the wild shrubbery and tangled vines enswathed by heavy clouds of smoke from the fires darkening the village, she and her friends escaped the brutality of the drunken mercenaries."

The house was rebuilt to grander elegance about 1793 for Thaddeus Burr by Daniel Dimon, a Fairfielder and well-known carpenter-architect. A huge colonial structure, it was modelled on the Hancock house in Boston and remained in the Burr family until the 1830s when it was sold and then owned by a succession of families until purchased by D.H. Warner. He enlarged it, enclosed the back sun parlor, and greatly increased the size of the gardens. The more than thirteen acres were magnificent, shaded by giant elms, with fields, orchards and vegetable gardens, as well as a formal garden with a fountain and covered

Fig Leaves and Fortunes

Warner's answer to the corsetless era of the 1920s was the Wrap-around.

pergola. An army of gardeners was needed to care for such an estate.

No doubt, D.H. was impressed by the history of the Burr mansion and proud of his ownership of such a treasure, but the purchase came at a particularly inopportune time. By the beginning of the twenties Warner Brothers was sinking. In the year 1921 sales dropped by a third and profits turned into a loss of over a million dollars as swollen inventories were marked down. The effect on surplus was mitigated by *writing up* the value of land, buildings, and machinery, thus permitting dividends to be continued at a cost of $345,000 per year. D.H. expected the troubles to be short-lived, and the other owners, who were mostly family members, needed the money. On October 21 of that year he wrote an optimisitic letter to his wife. "As far as Warner Brothers goes, we should come back with strength. We have gone through a hard period, but with revival of business we should go ahead." He believed the company could maintain its payment of common dividends and the preferred payments, he said, "were stable."

Unfortunately, his troubles were not short-lived. The "Jazz Age" and the "corsetless era," were upon him and the road to prosperity would be long and discouraging.

By 1922 Warner's sales were half what they were in 1920 and by 1931 less than a quarter, with profits nonexistent. Nevertheless, common dividends were paid until 1929 and preferred dividends until 1930. Such payments took their toll of the balance sheet in spite of occasional issuance of par-value capital stock to enhance the surplus. The resources of the company were being badly depleted.

It was not that the company management did not try to correct things. After all, they had no control of changing fashions. They could only hope to adapt their products to those changes. To do that, they had to design their products lighter and more comfortable and make sure thay conformed to the fashion dictate of "flat, straight, narrow, and boyish." They began by using more rubber. Woven elastic strips, two and three inches wide, were inserted at the top and bottom of the garments. So were elastic gores. The standard back or front-laced corset was abandoned in favor of the Corselette and the Wrap-around. The

The Twenties

former was an all-in-one style with shoulder straps to hold it up and hose supporters to hold it down. Little or much control could be built into it. The latter did away with laces, substituting horizontal stretch panels at the sides so that, as the advertising claimed, you could "wrap it and snap it" on. Even lighter garments followed: the Oriental, a particularly soft style that wrapped only about the hips and was promoted by a veiled model and the Shadow, a light, transparent girdle using double thicknesses of sheer voile.

But nothing worked; sales continued to fall. In 1931 they were under $2,500,000. By then, to make matters worse, the Great Depression had hit in full strength. Common shares on the New York Stock Exchange were worth only 11 percent of their 1929 value. Investors had lost $74 billion, three times the cost of World War I. More than 5,000 banks had failed. Over 270,000 familes had been evicted from their homes. Retail business in America's stores was at the abyss. No longer was it just the corset industry which was in trouble; now it was everybody. Bankruptcy was an alarming possibility for many firms, including Warner's. Its loss for the year 1931 was $242,157; for 1932, $192,085. By the end of the year 1932 its surplus was a *minus* $1,286,556. Its survival was doubtful.

All this was bad enough, but D.H. Warner was himself in trouble, no longer capable of managing the company. He had changed. Always a voluptuary, he had been able in his youth to successfully combine business with indulgence by means of his vast energy. As he grew older, his energies grew weaker, his urge for high living, stronger. He became fat and lazy, physically and mentally, drank too much, gave up exercise. By the late nineteen twenties he was a grotesque of his former self. His grandchildren, not having known him in his youthful prime, would remember him only as a corpulent old man, though he was only in his fifties or early sixties, smoking a big Cuban cigar, sitting in his over-stuffed armchair in the sun room of his magnificent Burr mansion in Fairfield or in the back seat of his open Locomobile, wearing an oversized coonskin coat, while his chauffeur, Jim Prescott, drove.

The company could, perhaps, have struggled better through D.H.'s deterioration if he had been willing to give authority to the group of capable younger executives whom he had hired and trained. This, unfortunately, he refused to do. While he was more and more away from the office at a time of crucial decisions, he did not make it possible for others to act in his absence. In addition, he insisted on drawing money out of the company through dividends and expenses at a time when it could hardly afford necessary business costs, let alone personal luxuries. While losing money and with a negative surplus, the company was still paying for his 105-foot yacht, *Trail* and for much of the cost of maintaining the Burr homestead, its grounds, and his "bungalow" on Greenfield Hill. A banker from New York's Chemical Bank came to review Warner Brothers at a time when the company was desperately seeking financial support. He first interviewed the younger management group and was favorably impressed, then was taken to D.H.'s home for a discussion with the chairman. There he found D.H. in his cups at noon. The banker's recommendation to his superiors was to have "nothing to do with Warner Brothers."

Unfortunately, D.H. was also a womanizer. In 1888 when he was twenty, he had married nineteen-year-old Maude Cady Winton in North Adams, Massachusetts. She came from a distinguished family, an attractive direct descendant of William Bradford, first governor of the Plymouth colony, and a daughter of a wealthy Oxford University graduate and newspaper editor. The marriage was the social event of the season. A special train from New York and Bridgeport carried hundreds of guests to the wedding, including the

D.H. Warner (far left) and his family in 1930. John Field is third from right in the back row, B.G. Warner is at the far right, and the author is next to D.H.

president of the New Haven railroad and P.T. Barnum. After the marriage she settled down in Bridgeport and later at the Burr mansion in Fairfield to a life of motherhood, charity, and society.

She was a gifted gardener, a founder and president of the Fairfield Garden Club. Of her the local newspaper commented, "She was a lover of nature and of gardens, and it was her pleasure to open her spacious estate for the spring and fall flower exhibits of the Fairfield Garden Club. Her gardens were the setting of many delightful social affairs . . . those who visited them sensed that they reflected her love of the outdoors and the beautiful." She was an officer of the staff of the children's ward of Bridgeport Hospital, a board member of the Associated Charities of Bridgeport, the Fairfield Welfare Association, and the Fairfield Visiting Nurses. She was loved and respected in the community, and her three children, DeVer, Margaret, and Bradford were devoted to her and she to them.

But her husband, especially as the years went by, gave her little joy. For him there was usually another woman; for her there was always a home to maintain, a place where she would receive him back when his current affair was over. She was forgiving and forgetting. Only once did her hidden anger rise to the surface. In 1924 she sued him for divorce, charging "intolerable cruelty." Once more he begged for forgiveness, and once more she agreed to forget. The suit was withdrawn.

She died of cancer in August 1931 at the age of sixty-two, and D.H., no longer protected by her presence, got into trouble immediately. Sometime before her death he had met a Mrs. Flora Martin, twenty years his junior, a native of California who had settled in Fairfield. Mrs. Martin, needing money, called on D.H. in his office and borrowed $366.

The Twenties

The two became friends, taking long automobile drives together and spending evenings at her house. He loaned or gave her jewelry and more than $120,000 in cash. Five weeks after Maude Cady Warner's death, he became engaged to Mrs. Martin and they were married within six months. None of the children, upset by the whole thing, attended the wedding.

In the opinion of the family, Mrs. Martin had married D.H. for his money, which, to her almost certain dismay and the surprise of the community, had been disappearing rapidly. The depression, the problems of the Warner Brothers Company, his extravagent style of living, now the gifts to his new wife (800 shares of Bridgeport Hydraulic, 400 of Bridgeport Gas Light, 35 of City-Trust, 116 of Warner Brothers, 110 of D.M. Read), all had eroded a once large estate. His children believed that she set out to get what was left. He began to drink more heavily, cut himself off from his children and grandchildren, appeared less frequently in his office, though he still held on to the facades of power. He wrote a series of wills, giving ever more of his remaining fortune to "Shotsie," as she was called.

On Sunday September 23, 1934, at the age of 66 he fell dead on his bedroom floor, the victim of what the doctor said was a heart attack. His latest will, written only four months before his death, gave the Burr homestead and all its books, paintings, family portraits, statues, silverware, china, and his former wife's jewelry to his new wife, granted her an immediate legacy of $25,000, and set up a $550,000 trust fund, from which she was to receive a minimum of $20,000 per year for life. The remainder of the estate was to go to his children. The trouble was that, after giving away the house and the furnishings, and setting up the trust fund, there was little money left.

It can be understood why the children were shocked by the terms of the will. After conferring together and with their lawyers, they decided to contest it on the grounds of "undue influence" exerted on their father by their stepmother. In apparent acknowledgement of her vulnerability to such a claim, Flora Warner signed an agreement giving back to the children half of the Burr homestead and half its contents and reducing her income from the trust to a yearly minimum of $13,000. The will was thus probated.

Six months later there erupted a bitter legal battle, which continued all the way to 1941, as Mrs. Warner sued the children, charging that she had been "very materially defrauded." Her lawyer, Hugh Alcorn, painted a picture of a widow so consumed by grief over the death of a beloved husband that she was willing to sign anything. To the probate judge he said, "The purpose of this court is to see that widows and orphans receive decent treatment. This reduction of Mrs. Warner's income does not give her sufficient to keep the property and feed her."

The trial quickly became a newspaper sensation as it wound its way from the Probate Court, to the Superior Court, to the Supreme Court of Errors, and back to the Superior Court:

"Blue-blood bankers, brokers, and lawyers stand shivering in their boots while the smart set is poised, waiting expectantly for the bombshells, in the sensational but weird war between the widow of the late D.H. Warner and her stepchildren."

"A parade of more than 20 bankers and brokers, who the widow claims co-operated in the scheme to cheat and defraud her, will be witnesses for her."

"Society will shiver. The Supreme Court has given Alcorn a lead that undoubtedly will expose the alleged machinations of those who Mrs. Warner claims co-erced her into signing away a large chunk of the fortune."

Fig Leaves and Fortunes

"Mrs. Warner declared she was told that Warner's children were saying their father was a drunkard and senile."

In the face of this barrage of adverse publicity the children at first reacted defensively and pushed their case. But as the years and the legal battle wore on, and after they had won in the Superior Court, but later when Flora Warner's request for an appeal had been granted, and another trial loomed, they did not have the heart to pursue the matter further. They signed an agreement giving Mrs. Warner substantially all she wanted. In any case, by then, the whole thing had become a tempest in a teapot, as D.H.'s assets had been largely wasted, and the arguments were over the remaining crumbs. The children never regained their family home with its historical heritage and its lovely gardens, their furniture, their family portraits, their mother's jewelry, or what was left of their family's fortune.

In these later years, when personal affairs of business leaders are regularly reported in the press, and seem to have little effect on corporate interests, it is perhaps difficult to understand why the sad ending to D.H. Warner's life should have so hurt Warner Brothers. But in those days, in the relatively small community of Bridgeport, where D.H. Warner had for so long been "Mr. Bridgeport," it certainly did. The company, teetering on the edge of disaster brought on by corsetless days, a great depression, poor management, and now family squabbles, faced a bleak future.

The man who saved Warner Brothers was D.H. Warner's son-in-law, John Field.

A Warner's ad of the 1920s featuring the Wrap-around.

The Twenties

7

The Thirties

*T*HE WORST year was 1933. In his inaugural address Franklin Roosevelt described
the situation. "Values have shrunk to fantastic levels; taxes have risen; our ability
to pay has fallen. . . . The withered leaves of industrial enterprise lie on every side; farmers find no markets . . . the savings of millions of families are gone . . . a host of unem-
ployed citizens face the grim problem of existence."

That was the bottom of the depression, and the recovery through the thirties was slow
and painful, marked by a recession in 1937 and the mounting specter of war. Hitler and
Mussolini were threatening Europe; the Sino-Japanese struggle began. The Austrian Ansch-
luss was less than a year later. Czechoslovakia was next, then Poland, and war was certain.

In such a decade the world of fashion, like the world itself, turned sober. Gone were
the extravagancies and eccentricities of the twenties. Gone were the straight figures, the
short, short skirts, the attempt of every woman to look like a man. Femininity and curves
were back; clothes were cut to fit at bust, waist, and hips. The *Pictorial Encyclopedia of
Fashion* reported "The silhouette of the clothes harmonized with the natural curves of the
female body." Foundation garments were designed to prevent bulges at any spot, yet thanks
to new fabrics were substantially lighter and firmer. Said *Vogue*, "Two and a half ounces —
that's the weight of the all-in-one on the scales — no more, in fact, than your pearls — skillful
designing has banished bulk; fabrics have become as light as webs, yet incredibly firm."

To understand the kind of man John Field was, it is necessary to go back to the fateful
summer of 1865, the summer Lee surrendered at Appomatox, Lincoln was shot, and the
summer when I. DeVer Warner was settling down as a country doctor in McGrawville and
Lucien C. Warner was graduating from Oberlin College. On June 25 of that year the little
hamlet of Viroqua, Wisconsin, was destroyed by a powerful tornado. A survivor wrote,
"When we saw the whirling mass coming on so swiftly, we went in all haste to the cyclone
cellar with death in view. The house above us trembled two or three seconds and then tipped
over and was crushed in the whirlwind. Our shelter gone, timbers were thrown upon us

and around us. Our home was soon emptied of its furniture; our position was a terrible one. My daughter was seated at the end of the shelf under which her mother had taken refuge, with her little one clinging to her for life. All was now in darkness. For one dreadful moment we were pierced with flying splinters, our eyes and hair filled with dust and pulverized plaster mixed with blood from our own bleeding scalps."

The "little one" was six year old Emma Tourgee who would become John Field's mother; the "daughter" was his grandmother, Sarah Carnelia Bennett Tourgee Williams; the writer was his great-grandfather, Charles Bennett. Of such rugged, pioneer stock did John Field come. At the age of ninety-three, in 1934, his grandmother, Cornelia, wrote a remarkable letter to him and his sisters describing her difficult early life and struggles to make a home in the West. "In my Vermont childhood there were seven children to be reared and educated. My parents could well see the income from the stony hillsides of their little farm would be inadequate and decided like Horace Greely to 'Go West.'

"As a part of the plan my sister, Harriet, fifteen years old, and I at twelve were sent to a boarding school at Springfield, Vermont, to cram an education in us to fit us for teachers in the great West with little conception of the difference between education in New England, where schools had flourished for a hundred years, and Wisconsin, just emerged from the Northwest Territory.

"In the meantime my father had been west to look over the conditions. We had relatives in Illinois who were shaking with fever and ague — malaria — and father preferred the woods and waters of Wisconsin and located his home in Hillsboro, later moving to Viroqua. At the same time he found schools for Harriet and me as lecturers in a nearby town.

"Instead of the select schools we expected, we found log school houses, home-made with pine desks and seats and children of all ages. Our principal text-book was *McGuffy's Reader*.

"We were making 15 or 20 dollars a month and lived with a Mr. and Mrs. Tourgee who had two grown sons and a little daughter. They were important people in the small community with a big farm and a big house over-flowing with hospitality. Falling in love with one of their sons, Charlie, was inevitable. I was only fifteen at the time so when I wrote my parents for consent to marry, my mother insisted I come home to find out if I was sane or not, and father took us home to Hillsboro early in the winter.

"In May Charles Tourgee came for me with a team of fine horses and buggy — the envy of the neighbors — and we were married at home by a Justice of the Peace, May 16, 1857. By then I was sixteen. In the meantime a little house had been built for us near the older Tourgee home.

"The first blow was the death of the dear Mother Tourgee, who had been so good to me and understood my youth and inexperience. She went suddenly, a victim of heart trouble. She never saw the dear baby, Emma, who was born the second year of our marriage. After Emma's birth, William, my husband's younger brother, began to complain of throat trouble, and tuberculosis ran its course rapidly, and at the time of his death it was apparent that Charlie would soon follow him. Finally the old home took us all in, and his father and I cared for Charlie to the end. My senses were so numbed with grief and weariness I can remember little of that death and burial. My little Emma was only two and a half years old."

Cornelia's father came to take her and Emma home to Viroqua, where they all survived the tornado. In time, she went to work as a clerk in her father's office and later married

The Thirties

Howard Williams, a local shoe store owner. But she never forgot those earlier days. "I had come to Viroqua empty-handed — so shorn of pride and ambition that it mattered little to me that I had no widow's weeds, not even a good black dress. But with returning hope and vigor I began to realize I was only twenty years old and competent, and that there was a place for me in this busy little village of Viroqua, which I have tried to fill more or less successfully for 73 years."

Cornelia, John Field's grandmother, died January 23, 1935, at the age of ninety-four, just three months after completing this letter.

John Field's paternal grandfather, Albert Field, was born in Falmouth, Maine, and, like the Doctors Warner, had to help his mother operate their small farm after his father's early death. His wife, Angeline, worked in a cotton mill until their marriage, and together they were desperately poor. One of John Field's sisters recalled, "I heard my grandmother tell how my grandfather had to go barefooted, walking over the salt marshes, to go for the cows in the late fall in order to save his shoes for colder weather." Of her grandmother she remembers, "She was a tiny woman who weighed less than 100 pounds. She seemed stern to me, but they said she was gentle and thoughtful of others. She always wore a dark gray close-fitting dress which was buttoned to the neck and reached the floor. This wool dress was stark and unbecoming. Her gray hair was parted in the middle and pulled back flat on the sides with a knot at the back. The only times I can remember seeing her sit down was when she was in church."

Not being able to make a living on their scraggly Maine farm, the Albert Field family moved west in 1851 to what they hoped was more fertile country in Wisconsin. Bringing their own load of lumber with them, they built a shanty in Hillsboro, the first house in what was then a new pioneer village. Later, when Albert's financial prospects were improving, they constructed a solid log home. He proved to be an able businessman, shrewd and calculating. Starting out as a stock farmer, he branched out into lumbering and real estate, and in the absence of a town bank, acted as a loan resource for newly arrived immigrants from the east. Within some years he was a local power and the owner of over 2,000 acres of land in and around Hillsboro.

Those who knew Albert respected him for his accomplishments, but were sometimes rebuffed by his sternness. He faithfully attended church every Sunday, always wearing a frock coat. At home on Sundays, the curtains were drawn, no games were played, and little or no cooking was done. It was said he was devoted to Angeline but was not always gentle with her, having a sharp temper and being irritable at times.

Cornelia's "little one" of the tornado was Emma, John Field's mother, and Walter, Albert Field's son, was his father. Walter graduated from the University of Wisconsin in 1878 and from its law school two years later. That year Emma and Walter were married and settled down in Viroqua, he to practice law, and she to raise a family of three daughters, Eva, Ruth, and Louella, and one son, John. Eva remembered the house where they lived. "The dining room was a combination kitchen and family room. The large black cast-iron stove served to cook the food, heat the house, and warm the water. A hand pump was in the corner of the pantry with an older pump out back. There was a cyclone cellar under the house with a door leading to it from the outside. The Victorian house was complete with ferneries in the parlor. Also in the parlor were red horse-hair chairs and sofas and dark lacy woodwork whatnots. Our family amused itself with stereoptician slides of the Wild West and old picture albums."

John was born in this house in 1886 and was only three years old when his father, at times a restless adventurer, heard the call of an even wilder west and rushed to claim his share of federally unassigned lands in Oklahoma when it was first opened to non-Indian settlement, thus joining the thousands of men and women running for new property and new hope in a new territory.

After Walter laid claim to land in Oklahoma City, he brought Emma and their children to homestead there. They first lived in a house made of sod before building another Victorian structure remarkably similar to the one they had left in Wisconsin. In Oklahoma Walter as a practicing lawyer was busy representing local Indians in their claims against the U. S. Government and in going into the dry goods business with a partner named Oscar Mitscher. This was the father of Mark Mitscher, a life-long friend of the Field family, who was destined to be famous in World War II as Commander of Naval Task Force 38.

Unfortunately the retail business in Oklahoma City was not successful, and restlessness again moved Walter, his wife, and their children to a new place — this time, Washington D.C., where he started his own law practice, represented the Isbrandson Moller Steamship Company of New York, and looked after certain Indian interests in the nation's capital. But, still a westerner by heart, in the city he missed the openness of his remembered farmland and the feel of the good earth beneath his feet. To assuage his longings, he purchased a small garden plot on the edge of town where he could work the land and grow a few crops. It was there, while digging in a cold, spring rain, that he contracted pneumonia and died on April 24, 1925.

Meanwhile his son, John, was growing up. A rugged, strong, handsome, young man, it was said he bore considerable resemblance in looks and manner to his grandfather, Albert. Like him he was pragmatic, decisive, opinionated, and impatient. And in some ways he was like his maternal grandmother, Cornelia. He had her resourcefulness, her ability to survive disasters. At Washington's Eastern High School he was an outstanding football player and through friends applied for, and was accepted, at Yale University. His college career, while not noted for academic brilliance, proved his relish for hard work and his dogged determination to succeed. He was a first baseman on the junior varsity baseball team, an oarsman in the Yale crew, and, most important, the starting fullback on the Yale football team and a nationally acclaimed super-star. Many years later his oldest son remembered, "I was a second-string quarterback on the Yale freshman football team. It was a bitter cold day, the ground frozen with just a top layer of mud, and we were having live tackling practice, which exercise I hated. Needless to say, I badly missed the man I was supposed to tackle, and as I pulled myself out of the mud, aching and resentful, I heard one old Yale graduate on the sidelines say to another old Blue, 'Don't tell me that's Johnny Field's son. His old man never tackled like that!'"

It was during his senior year that John Field met D.H. Warner. John had a friend, Robert Gibney, business manager of the Yale News, who had been hired to work for Warner's after graduation and who thought it would be pleasant to have John with him. On January 9, 1911, Bob wrote to D.H. recommending John for a position at Warner's. "In regards to John's character, it is one of the finest I know, and his ability to keep working at whatever he takes up is recognized throughout college. He says he wants work which will keep him going hard all the time with a chance for advancement if he makes good. He will work with every bit of energy in him." Bob Gibney knew John Field well.

The Thirties

There was one difficulty for John in going to work immediately for Warner's after graduation. He had an offer from Amherst College to coach its football team for $1,500 and he needed the money. This problem was resolved when he received a similar offer to coach the Yale team for the 1911 fall season, and D.H. Warner offered him a position with enough latitude to do both the Warner's and Yale jobs. For the rest of his life he would remain absorbed in Yale football. It sometimes seemed that nothing was more important to him than the fate of the Yale team. On many autumn afternoons he could be found at Yale football practice, and on Saturday he was always present, sun, rain, or snow, at that week's game. Virtually every Monday morning until his death he wrote a letter to a succession of Yale coaches critiquing the weekend's proceedings. To what extent the coaches appreciated these frequent letters, or whether they paid any attention to them, is not known. Carm Cozza, the present coach, says that *he* liked getting them and that they were very helpful.

When D.H. Warner hired John Field, he did not know he was not only employing a future chief executive but a son-in-law as well. D.H.'s daughter, Margaret ("Peg" to her father and close friends) had met John earlier at a Yale prom and thought him the "handsomest man I had ever seen and the best dancer." His first job with Warner's was helping D.H. with his political and community activities outside the company. This assignment brought him frequently to the Warner homes. Years later he remembered driving his motorcycle up Greenfield Hill on the muddy, rutty dirt road that then connected that rural area with downtown Fairfield and Bridgeport, where he lived as a bachelor at the University Club. Acquaintance with Margaret blossomed into love, and the two were married at the colonial Greenfield Hill Congregational Church in September of 1913.

By the years of the depression John Field had served his apprenticeship well, having worked at every job in the company, except that of salesman. He had even spent a couple of years abroad right after World War I when L.T. Warner, with an interest in developing a Warner's business in Europe, had started what turned out to be an unsuccessful sewing plant in Belgium. In all those years he had been a loyal supporter of D.H. though chafing under the dictatorial rule and indolence of the chairman. Reward for his patience came in 1929 when he was elected president, though he still had to endure a few years of frustration as D.H. Warner countermanded and upset his plans, and it was not until after D.H.'s death that he was able, as chief executive officer, to really take charge.

By then the company's problems were monumental. For years there had been no profits, and the outlook for the future was no better. To see the company through the difficult times ahead, it needed solid banking help, which it did not have. The Chase Bank, long its major lender, had just withdrawn its support. One of the major obstacles to better bank relations was an 8 percent cumulative preferred stock whose dividends were far in arrears and whose presence severely weakened the balance sheet. No progress could be made until this debt was removed. In a brave letter to the holders of that preferred, dated December 14, 1933, the company, at the instigation of John Field, asked the preferred holders to voluntarily forgive their unpaid back dividends and to take in place of the old preferred a choice of two new non-cumulative preferreds at 3 percent per year. The letter acknowledged that radical changes in women's dress had affected the company seriously and "in addition the present long continued depression has followed with consequences beyond any modern precedent." Furthermore, preferred stockholders had been paid dividends when earnings were insufficient to do so, and thus "were paid out of capital belonging to the holders of common stock. Some dividends were even paid at the personal expense of one

Fig Leaves and Fortunes

or more of the company's officers."

The acceptance by the stockholders of this proposal (they really had no alternative) marked the beginning of the recovery. New bank accounts were opened with solid institutions such as the Guaranty Trust Company and the Bank of Boston, both of whom pledged their support. Jobs were eliminated, expenses slashed, salaries cut, inventories reduced. D.H. Warner's yacht was sold, so were his fancy cars. A new regime of extreme austerity was imposed and its author and monitor was a tough John Field.

Fortunately for him and the company, the thirties at Warner's did produce a series of profitable product innovations, the result of collaboration between himself and a skilled designer named Alice Cromwell. In an article for the trade magazine, *Corset and Underwear Review*, John Field explained, "Women today must be comfortable. In the past, when corsets were made with little or no elastic, they were not only uncomfortable but injurious to health. Today they are made with more and more rubber."

To do this, new elastics and new ways to use them became the goal of Warner's designing. A constant woman's problem was holding the corset or girdle down on the hips. The "Great Feminine Gesture" was yanking down the girdle. A Warner's booklet explained, "Did you ever stop to think that your body lengthens through the back hips when you sit, stoop, or crouch?. . . . Some figures lengthen as much as four inches. A cloth back corset rides up and has to be pulled down."

The solution for this was an elastic fabric that stretched up and down as well as around the body. But could it be done? The people from U.S.Rubber thought so, and after considerable experimentation found a way to do so. To Warner's they brought a few yards of a new fabric that was soft, thin, and stretched *both ways*. The girdles made from the new fabric got glowing reviews: "most comfortable garment I ever wore . . . it never hikes up . . . fits like a second skin." The tiny thread was "Lastex"*; the fabric that was perfected from it was "Youthlastic"; and the product made of this fabric was Warner's "LeGant" (French for "the glove").

But a problem remained: the new LeGants, stretching as they did both up and down and around, while comfortable, did not give the control over the hips many women wanted. Fashion in the early thirties called for flat hips, and LeGants tended to round the hips. The solution was "Two-Way-One-Way." This design combined two-way stretch panels over the hips with a panel stretching *only vertically* in the back or in the back and front. Here was a garment employing panels at the side stretching around the body with panels at the back and front *not stretching around the body*, but with all of the panels stretching *up and down*, so that the corset could stretch with the movements of the body and yet stay in place . . . and flatten the hips.

These two-way stretch fabrics could be made so light and soft that they were even used in the cup portion of bras. Warner's called their elastic, stretchable bras "Alure." It was Warner's also who first made ABC sizing in bras. Different women had different sizes of breasts. Warner's ABC bras, introduced in 1935, were sized A for small bust, B for average bust, C for heavy bust, and D for very heavy bust. This classification assured the wearer of better fit, and more than doubled brassiere sales, not only for Warner's, but for the entire industry, which quickly followed Warner's lead in bra sizing.

Meanwhile, the soft unboned two-way stretch or "Two-Way-One-Way" girdle still had

*A trademark of Uniroyal.

The Thirties

1930s advertisement for the revolutionary Warner's Le Gant.

Fig Leaves and Fortunes

one fault: it had a tendency to roll over at the waistline. In January of 1938 an astute inventor, named Henry Herbener, brought to Warner's his patented elastic waistband stiffened with featherweight bones. With it Warner's designers produced the "Sta-Up-Top" girdle, which did not roll over at the waist. Its success was immediate.

L.T. Warner, now chairman of the board, and still in charge of advertising and international, wasted no time in promoting these new products with his usual imagination. Girdle ads depicted a woman wearing a LeGant standing, sitting, or crouching, all in perfect comfort, as well as swimming, skating, golfing, and using a bow and arrow. Most spectacularly a corset fashion show was staged once a year during the fall market week in New York. Originally the show, which used live models and dramatized the close relationship between undergarments and dress fashions, was presented to retail buyers and executives at the Warner's office at 200 Madison Ave. Gradually, however, the show became so popular it had to be moved to larger quarters, first at the Hotel McAlpin, then at the Astor, and finally in 1941 to the Grand Ballroom of the Waldorf Astoria, where an audience of 1,500 watched a theatrical performance in ten acts with an orchestra, songs, elaborate scenery and forty models. Warner's had become the Billy Rose of the corset industry.

Even Warner's bankers came to the show, more out of curiosity probably than for enlightenment. Lewis Shay, president of the Connecticut National Bank, muttered as he sat in the front row, "This show is a bust!"

It was also during the thirties that L.T. made progress in developing an international business for Warner's. Some of the company's new products were protected by patents or by well-known brand names, both of which had appeal abroad. In Great Britain he established Warner's own company with its own designing and selling, but with contract manufacturing. In other countries, including France, Germany, Sweden, Belgium, Spain, Argentina, Mexico, and Brazil he licensed local manufacturers to design and sell Warner's products.

Through his contacts in France L.T. also met the celebrated dress designer Mainboucher, who at the time believed that women were tired of the somewhat drab fashions of the thirties and would like to return to the more romantic, pre-World War I look of a narrower waist and high bustline. His own dress designs were moving in that direction, but he needed the right foundation garments to go with them. L.T. offered to supply such styles, and the result was a line of Mainboucher-Warner foundation garments, not only reflecting the designer's ideas of waist and bust but also being made in eye-catching colors and polkadots instead of the old-fashioned pink or white.

They were a sales disaster. Customers, at least American customers, did not understand or appreciate such radical looking underwear. John Field, who always had difficulty relating to novel ideas, said he had known all along "they would be turkeys." They confirmed his belief that fashion was not a reliable indicator for foundation garment design. Actually, though John Field would never acknowledge it, Mainboucher was simply ahead of his time. Right after the war Christian Dior introduced the same idea of a slimmer waistline and a higher bustline, and it was a world-wide success. In a letter to his English manager, John Field warned him not to "invest one dollar in the Mainboucher stuff, because we are dropping the whole scheme. The Mainboucher name is mud in this country."

In any case the English manager, J. Herbert Lewis, would not have had time to launch the Mainboucher promotion before the start of the European war in September 1939. His

The Thirties

Warner's fashion show at the Waldorf Astoria in New York in the early 1940s.

Fig Leaves and Fortunes

was the first Warner company to be hit by German bombs, which rocked its offices and factories. He wrote from London, "The West End has suffered considerably the last few days, and although the office is surrounded by damaged buildings, apart from a few broken windows, our building is still intact. Three of the girls on the staff live outside of London, and it is impossible for them to get into town. Jack, one of our juniors, had a lucky escape when his house was hit and completely demolished. Miss Essex has been evacuated from her house because of a time bomb in her garden. Mr. Randall had excitement when a large oil bomb fell on his block, and his flat is sodden with water. Everybody has had bombs drop very close. It is frightening."

The drama of the German advance was pictured in a letter received by L.T. from Leon Laloyaux, the Warner's licensee for France and Belgium. "Upon the approach of the German armies, we did as everybody in Belgium tried to do. We went to France by auto, abandoning everything — our houses, our stores, our factory, carrying with us enough food to last a few days and money for a month. At the French frontier, at Tournai, my son found himself in the middle of a bombardment, which destroyed half the city and his car. When we arrived in the Pas-de-Calais region we were overtaken by German troops and prevented from going any further. After twenty-eight days we were able to return to Brussels, after having passed many nights in the cars, in the open fields, or on straw like nomads. Once, a little later, our son Henri almost lost his life. His train was attacked by planes and cut in three pieces. There were many wounded and killed but Henri got out safely from under the cars. I myself (having returned to Belgium) have had the good luck of not being disturbed by the occupying Nazis, undoubtedly because of my age. Nevertheless, I have always been alert for you know that in the war of 1914-1918 I was put in prison for spying, and everyone knows that the Germans never forget."

In spite of the Mainboucher set-back, Warner's by the forties had slowly emerged from its own and the nation's depression. From sales in 1931 of $2,427,949 and a loss of $242,157, the figures had begun to improve. Even though sales had dropped farther by 1933, to $2,276,541, a miniscule profit of $6,621 appeared. By 1937 sales were up to $2,916,869 and profit to $184,896; by 1941 sales topped $4 million and the profit was over $300,000.

By the time war came to the United States, John Field had matters at Warner Brothers well under control. If he thought that he personally was in an unusual situation — a rugged, western individualist, a football-playing descendant of poverty-stricken pioneers — leading a business selling women's undergarments for a third-generation family of eastern gentry — he confided in no one.

Away from the office John and his wife, Margaret, were busy with an active social life and raising their three children. The author of this history, I was the oldest, born in 1914, while my brother, William (Bill), and my sister, Jean, followed in 1917 and 1919.

Just before World War I John and Margaret were living in a modest home on Park Avenue in Bridgeport, only a block or so from the Warner's plant. From there he could walk to and from work every day. It was there too, at home, that I was born, the event, as was the custom in those times, being supervised by a doctor and a midwife. It was not many years later, however, that with my father's growing importance in the company we moved to a larger house in Brooklawn Park, one of the area's first suburban real estate developments, actually located in Fairfield just below the Brooklawn Country Club, of which my great-grandfather, Dr. I. DeVer Warner, as mentioned before, had been a founder.

In Brooklawn Park we lived in relative affluence. At some time during World War I, while driving one of the new-fangled cars on behalf of the Red Cross, my mother had a rendezvous with a construction site in Bridgeport, hooking on to and dragging a clattering-wheel barrow down Main Street pursued by a screaming mob of workmen. On another occasion she drove her car to the Brooklawn club, but forgetting how to stop the machine, drove round and round the circle in front of the main entrance until, witnesses attested, she crashed into the side of the club. As the result of several such incidents my father had forbidden her to drive any more and had hired a chauffeur. He said it was for her own protection, and incidentally, for the protection of others.

The chauffeur was soon joined by a cook, a maid, a nurse for the children, and a man to take care of the outdoors, all of whom, as again was the custom in those days, being at least partially paid by Warner Brothers. The result was that Bill, Jean, and I were often cordoned off from our mother and father, being confined to our bedrooms, the kitchen, and the maids' dining room where we ate many of our meals while our parents entertained their friends, both personal and business, in the main part of the house.

My mother was an intelligent woman with an artistic and literary flair, but self-centered and spoiled by both her father and her husband, whom she loved with a commanding jealousy. Somewhat of a hypochondriac, she had breakfast in bed every day of her adult life, was driven by the chauffeur to her shopping, her afternoon meetings, teas, and bridge. Her interests lay in her friends, her charitable work, the Junior League, for whom she wrote plays, the Fairfield Garden Club, and the Thursday Thimble Club, of which she was a charter member. Asked why she never missed a meeting of the latter group, she would answer, "If you don't attend, they will talk about you."

My father was quite different: strict, demanding, intense, a strange mixture of sternness and kindness. Many were the scoldings for minor offenses; many the whippings with the back of a hairbrush for major offenses, especially for me, the oldest. I was sent to public school while my brother and sister attended private school. At his command I walked the long road to school every day in all kinds of weather. He insisted I earn money with a paper route, yet when I was sick, he himself distributed my papers. When my friends and I organized a football team, he hired a young man from Yale to coach us. At Christmas he dressed as Santa Claus.

Especially in the early days we had many good times with him. He loved outdoor sports like fishing, hunting, golf, and sailing, and rented a camp in the Adirondacks where we learned something about the woods, the lakes, and the hills, and when we were a little older, he took us fishing in Canada. We always owned a sailboat or two and all of us became reasonably adept at racing them.

Most important, he gave us a good education. Even in the dark days of the depression, when Warner's was tottering, he somehow found money to pay our tuitions at top-flight schools. Wherever we were, however, he found it difficult to praise us or even show warmth over any of our accomplishments. When I was elected to Phi Beta Kappa in Junior Year at Yale or won the Francis Gordon Brown prize for "intellectual ability, high manhood, and capacity for leadership and service" there was no word from him. Instead, when I overran my allowance (as my uncle D.C. Warner had done a generation before) and was threatened with expulsion from college for nonpayment of a tuition bill, he refused to help. When

I was first arrested for speeding in an automobile, he told the judge to "throw the book" at me.

When I graduated from college in the recession year of 1937, foolishly turning down a Yale offer of a scholarship at Cambridge University in England because I wanted to get to work immediately, I was lucky enough to find a position with Time Inc. in New York. My father did not offer me a job at Warner's, nor would I have accepted one if it had been offered. I did not want to work for him, and making corsets and brassieres was, at that time, my idea of the height of ignominy.

I was happy that I had taken the New York job. It was a great place to be then, just before the war, and I had a wonderful time. In April of 1939 I married Priscilla Brown, a beautiful girl from Wilmington, Delaware, whom I had met on a Southern vacation during college. We had an apartment in Forest Hills with a living room, bedroom, and kitchen, for which we paid $60 per month. Inasmuch as I was now making $60 *a week*, the world was our oyster. We were in heaven.

On December 3, 1941, the largest Warner's Fashion Show in history was held at the Waldorf-Astoria. Four days later the Japanese attacked Pearl Harbor. A week later our first child, Margaret, was born. Shortly after Christmas I found myself on the Matson ocean liner *Lurline* in San Francisco Bay along with 5,000 sailors and shipyard workers, bound, as a reporter, for Hawaii and the war.

Mr. and Mrs. DeVer Howard Warner
request the honour of
Mr. and Mrs. Hamilin's
presence at the marriage of their daughter
Margaret Lucetta
to
Mr. John Field
on Tuesday, the twenty-third of September
at four o'clock in the afternoon
at the Greenfield Hill Church
Fairfield, Connecticut

The Thirties

8

The Forties

THE WAR was over. For those who had served overseas, gone were the long days of loneliness and boredom, the sudden terror. For those who stayed home, gone were the interminable days of waiting. For all it was a time of homecoming, of picking up the tangled threads of disrupted lives.

In fashion's realm gone too were the days of clothes rationing, the ersatz materials, the drab styles of wartime. In a sudden explosion of creativity designers once more luxuriated in satins, silks, laces, embroideries, and especially in that new and miraculous fibre developed by DuPont—nylon. For the corset trade real rubber returned. In Paris Christian Dior, understanding that women everywhere were yearning for something new and more feminine, launched his "New Look," a nipped-in waist, a rounded, more prominent bosom, a lower decollete, a longer skirt. Fashion excitement was everywhere. British *Vogue* reported breathlessly, "There are moments when fashion changes fundamentally . . . this is one of those moments."

Nevertheless, America faced the postwar years with uncertainty. Only the coming of war had lifted the nation out of its decade-long depression. Would not the end of war production mean a resumption of that depression? John Field thought it probably would.

He need not have worried. Business boomed in the late forties as consumer demand, so long restrained by wartime shortages and controls, burst out in a wave of buying. Warner's too flourished. As early as 1947 sales hit almost $12 million, and profits were just short of one million. Times were very good.

Back at *Life* magazine, I was suffering a kind of postwar petulance. It had been all right during the war when I was busy reporting from abroad, or at home from interviews and research. Toward the end I had been promoted to national affairs editor and concentrated on politics, but I was not sure what the future held. I was going about my assignments with a certain lassitude and lack of interest. I needed a change.

Priscilla and I now had two children (John had been born in 1944), and we were finding New York an uncomfortable place in which to bring them up. For a brief while we tried living in the country, in Westport, Connecticut, but the New York commute was long and arduous, especially with the uncertain hours of a news magazine. I came down with ulcers, and we promptly moved back to New York, within walking distance of the office.

One lovely Sunday afternoon in the early spring of 1946, feeling melancholy, we took the children, baby carriage and all, for a walk in Central Park, stopping for a rest on a little sward of greening grass. Along came a New York policeman.

"Get off the grass," he barked, "before I put you under arrest."

"But officer," I pled, "we are not harming the grass."

"That's the law, buddy. Get moving!"

That did it. We agreed we could no longer live in New York, a place where our children could not even play on the grass. That evening I called my father to tell him we were leaving New York to go somewhere else, almost anywhere else. I was only thirty-one, had the opportunity for an editing job on a newspaper in Nebraska, an offer from a magazine in California. There were some people who might help me buy the local Fairfield paper. He suggested, instead, that I come to work for Warner's; he would pay me 25 percent *less* than I was making at *Life* but we would be in the country. All too hastily I accepted, reckoning that expenses in Connecticut would be at least 25 percent under what they were in New York and that even with a lower income we would live more comfortably, and not be told to get off the grass.

Going to work for my father proved to be an unfortunate mistake, as I should have known, and I believe that he too always regretted hiring me. We were such different people. I should have remembered that he had grown up in a frontier community, to hard times, that it had taken determination and tenacity for him to rescue a company in desperate plight. He was tough, pragmatic, a staunch conservative, nonintellectual, intolerant of others, superb in detail, confiding and trusting in nobody. His concept of organization was to have everybody report to him. For him everything was black or white, never grey. He did not waste time in debates with himself; he always knew what was right or wrong. Working successfully for him required subservience.

Once I was with him on a slow boat to Labrador for salmon fishing. We had two days to talk. I said I would like to discuss some ideas I had. He was not interested. "Why bother? I know what you think. I know what I think. We are not going to change each other. Let's talk about fishing."

I grew up in a softer world—a world of pleasant homes, of golf, tennis, and sailing, of prep schools and Ivy League colleges. For ten years I had made a good living as a writer and reporter. Imaginative, sentimental, a reader, dreamer and worrier, politically a liberal, impatient with detail, I was everything he was not. He was everything I was not.

But there was one thing we had in common: a stubborn determination to run our own show. Each of us wanted to be boss; conflict between us was inevitable. The normal confrontation to be expected in any company between old and new management styles was to be aggravated, in this case, by a difficult father-son relationship.

Disagreement came earlier than either of us had expected. By the time of my arrival at the company, L.T. Warner, the immensely popular chairman, was gradually retiring from an active managerial role. Most of his days were spent out of the office devoting time to his three major interests: Oberlin College where he had been a trustee since 1915, the United Congregational Church which he joined in 1905 and where he was senior deacon, and the

YMCA where he had held almost every office, local and national, since 1904. He was also a trustee of the People's Savings Bank, a director of the Bridgeport Hydraulic Company and of Bridgeport Hospital. He and my father had developed an understanding: one would run the business, the other would take care of the company's civic and charitable interests. My father liked this arrangement because it left him unmistakably in charge of Warner's. When L.T. died on March 5, 1950, he left a legacy of good works. His only secretary over all the years, Theresa Haggeman, worshipped him. "His contacts with important and interesting people made working for Mr. Warner far more than merely a means of earning a living. He measured up to the highest standards of a gentleman and an American."

In the few short years I knew him, I grew very fond of L.T. As he gradually retired, I was given the job of taking over supervision of advertising from him, although, like everybody else, I reported, not to him, which I would have enjoyed, but directly to my father. Promptly, as might have been expected, my father and I disagreed on what kind of advertising was best for Warner's. I thought the company's ads, which used photographs of models on whom the details of the foundation garments were sketched literally with an etching pencil, were old-fashioned and in bad taste. Every line, every bone, every decoration, were clearly drawn. The result was popular with the salesmen, with the stores' corset buyers, and with my father because each style could be clearly identified and distinguished from any other style. But I was convinced they had little popular appeal. His old college classmate, Bob Gibney, who had worked briefly for Warner's and then gone into the advertising business, still ran the company's agency. Dissatisfied with his creativity, I hired a new agency headed by Chester J. LaRoche, a former president of Young and Rubicam. Promptly Warner's art and copy took on a youthful, high-style air, far more appropriate, I believed, for a fashion company. A photographer whose work usually appeared in *Vogue* or *Harper's Bazaar* shot softly lit models in typical boudoir scenes wearing Warner's styles on which most of the detail was lost. The headlines were gay and whimsical and frequently involved a play on words. "You Ought to be Hugged, not Squeezed." "You'll look so Naughty, Feel so Nice." "Darling, We'd like to put our Charms around You." The intention was to associate Warner's with good taste, gentle femininity, and a sense of humor.

John Field did not like these ads, but he allowed us to use them, partly at least because L.T. approved of them. The Daniel Starch Organization, which measured readership and noting of advertisements, reported that the new ads performed at 100 percent above average. *Advertising and Selling* magazine called the first new Warner's ad the "outstanding lingerie ad of the month" and *Tide* magazine picked the headline "You Ought to be Hugged, not Squeezed" as "the outstanding headline of the month among all national advertisers." Most importantly, sales skyrocketed.

With our new agency and our new advertising we found ourselves closer than ever to the fashion designers, both here and in Paris. Dior's "New Look" had changed the cut and shape of women's dresses, but in my opinion, and in the agency's opinion, Warner styling had not changed with it. We were still doing the bulk of our business in pre-war LeGants, Sta-Up-Tops, and Half-Size corselettes. That was all right, because they were basic merchandise for us, and foundation garment styles do not change fast, but we needed something new to be worn with the new fashions, something innovative, something to catch the attention of the fashion world. To get it, one of our ablest designers conceived what became our famous "Merry Widow," a combination waist-cinch, garter belt, and half-bra. Its highly successful launching was tied into the release of a Lana Turner movie of Franz

Fig Leaves and Fortunes

You ought to be hugged...not squeezed!

How Warner's miracle 3-Way-Sizes bring you heavenly comfort through heavenly fit

Warner's exclusive 3-Way-Sizes make "standard sizing" as old-fashioned as your Aunt Matilda.

• Twins may be the same height and weight—yet need different girdle lengths. Warner's* foundations come in four lengths: short, medium, long and extra long.

• In addition to your own length, Warner's come in three hip sizes, too; straight, average and full.

• What's more, from over 200 styles and sizes you can select fabrics and designs to give you just the control you want.

• If you want to lose inches without feeling pinches, get the Warner's that's "individually yours"—3 ways.

Sta-Up-Top Warnerette #634, in white, pink, blue, $5.00. Extra large, $6.50

In your size... *your correct length*

Ever get a girdle that's *too long* . . . makes you hobble? Or a "*too short*" that pulls at your precious nylons? Not in a Warner's. They're sized; short, medium, long and extra long. The Sta-Up-Top® Warnerette® above features Warner's famous patented waistband that won't roll over.

your correct hip size

Hip, hip AWAY! Wonderful—but it never happens in a girdle that's *too wide* and forms gaping pockets at the sides. Or one that's *too small* and binds your thighs. You'll find a Warner's that's *just right*—they're *hip-sized*; straight, average and full.

your choice of control

For tummy-tucking there's a Warner's to give you just the control you want. For example, the Warnerette illustrated is especially designed for little figures that don't add up to much. For a lot of control, you'll find a Warner's that inches you in—but comfortably. *At finer shops and stores everywhere.*

Girdles · Corselettes
Pantie Girdles · Bras

WARNER'S

Reg. U. S. Pat. Off.

WORLD FAMOUS FOR LE GANT® · STA-UP-TOP® · ABC® ALPHABET® · REDFERN®

First new style Warner's advertisement after World War II. It won headline-of-the-month award among all national advertisers in 1948.

The Forties

Lehar's operetta, because it actually did resemble the old-fashioned, tight-waisted, corset worn in the days of the *Merry Widow*, and incidentally in the early days of the doctors Warner. It was perfect for the new Diors.

Unfortunately, we were never able to take full advantage of the excitement caused by the Merry Widow and by other fashion items such as the "Cinch," another style for the Dior look that gently pulled in the waist. My father, skeptical of fashion, refused to allow the factories to make many of these new styles. "Just gimmicks," he argued, "Will not sell. Will be inventory mark-downs. Remember Mainboucher. Stick to basics."

He was wrong. The new styles were outstanding successes, featured in newspapers, fashion magazines, and even in *Time* and *Newsweek*, and the orders from stores cascaded in. But because of the delay in getting started, we were not able to gear up our production fast enough to fill all our orders before our competitors had put *their* versions of the same styles on the market, and it was they who reaped much of the volume and the profits.

The new advertising and the new styles illustrated the difference in thinking between my father and myself. The ads and the merchandise were modern and fashion-right, but a consumer survey, taken in 1947, showed that, in spite of the innovations, women associated Warner's mostly with old-fashioned corsets for the heavy figure. They did not know that throughout its history the firm had been a pioneer in fashion design.

To change this image, we needed a marketing plan to promote the "new Warner's." Advertising and innovative styling were not enough. The company as a whole had to learn that advertising was only part of marketing's assignment to move goods from the manufacturer's shelves through the retail stores to the final customers. This required professional market research both before and after the design, production, and sale of the product, plus reorder systems to keep the goods in stock on retail shelves. Other needed tools were educated and informed salesmen, store tie-in advertising, sales training, and window and departmental displays.

All this was difficult. Because of the intimate nature of our product and the fact that the corset department, even if badly run, produced one of the highest, if not the highest, profit in their stores, retail managers tended to leave the corset buyer alone. In turn, she often became a prima donna, queen in her own domain. For years this buyer domination had prevented modern merchandising methods from getting more than the barest toe-hold in the nation's girdle and bra departments.

What was required was the establishment of a working partnership between a manufacturer such as Warner's and its retail distributors. Some of our competitors were doing a better job at this than we were. Unfortunately for us, Warner's sales managers and salesmen, trained in the old school and afraid of their buyers, were hesitant to learn modern marketing and especially to go over the heads of their buyers to store management. I wrote my father, "Up to now we have been primarily concerned with our salesmen selling the buyers our styles. This is still important. But we must now also be concerned with moving our line through the stores. This means selling the stores on the profitability of Warner's merchandise so that they will give us the in-store push we need. We must reach, not only the buyer, but also the divisional merchandise manager, the general merchandise manager, and the promotion departments, including advertising, display, and fashion coordinators. Our salesmen must learn how a corset department is run. They must have facts and figures on turnover, mark-ups, mark-downs, margins, operating results, display and

You'll look so naughty—feel so nice in WARNER'S

Warner-Wonderful for New Year's Eve — or any eve when you want to look a *little* wanton! It's the one, the only — the *original* Cinch-bra that took the country by storm.

Takes as much as two inches from your waist! Shapes the most bewitching curves with comfy wires *under* the bust so the sheer bra cuffs can dip *surely*, sensationally low.

See for yourself. *Everything nice* happens to the girl who starts her holidays in Warner's Merry Widow! In misty black or white nylon marquisette and elastics, #1311 at $12.50.

And the more the *merrier!* Look for a whole family of Warner's styles, inspired by this fabulous flatterer—strapless bras to lacy corselettes. Now at your nicest stores, here and in Canada.

WARNER'S
*REG. U. S. PAT. OFF.

Bras · Girdles · Corselettes

In much the same vein . . . advertisement for Warner's famous Merry Widow circa 1950.

The Forties

advertising techniques, copy appeal, results of promotional efforts, analysis of department locations and stock control methods. They must help merchants earn more money on their corset departments and in so doing, convince them of the importance of making Warner's their top and basic line."

All this would require education for our sales managers and their salesmen. But neither John Field nor the sales managers agreed. They still believed it safer to work solely with the store buyer, not with store management. "She's the one who writes the orders," they said. The result was lack of cooperation between our advertising department, operating under my direction, and our sales departments, operating under three separate regional sales managers individually reporting to my father. He, in turn, made it quite clear that he had little enthusiasm for our new ideas, and that without his support, they had no chance of being accepted.

Further problems arose because the sales organization had its own promotion and publicity departments separate and distinct from our advertising and under the control of the sales managers. These departments ran all style and fashion promotions, conducted corset fitting schools to train retail sales clerks, and staged large and small fashion shows, all directed at store buyers and store salesgirls. There was little reference in any of these activities to our national advertising, which some of the sales managers and salesmen felt we could do without. At a sales conference in Atlanta, one of our assistant sales managers asked me why we did not stop all "this nonsense of paying so much money for space in *Life* magazine," and instead give him a little extra money to "sprinkle around among my customers." In that case, he promised, he would show some "really big sales gains."

As early as December 1948 I was writing my father, "All the promotional and advertising activities should be centered under me. The result of our present system is ineptly divided effort and lack of coordination."

This memo was never answered. John Field did not like being told how to run *his* business, especially by a son who had been with the company for only two years.

From the perspective of many years later, I now can see that had I been in his shoes, I might well have felt the same as he did, even if I, the father, had been wrong and the son, right.

L.T. Warner

Fig Leaves and Fortunes

9

The Fifties

FOR THE NATION the 1950s began in disillusionment as the hopeful promise of postwar peace and harmony evaporated. The Korean War was unsettled and unpopular, McCarthyism rampant, the Truman administration tired and inept. The decade ended in turmoil and trouble: the beginning of a battle over Civil Rights, a hotter Cold War, anti-Americanism everywhere.

But in between there came the glorious honeymoon of the Eisenhower years as the country entered a period of serenity not seen since before World War I. Critics called it an age of conformity, the time of the "silent generation," of complacency and self-satisfaction. Probably all that was true. Certainly business was good, too good to last, but while it lasted, it was to be enjoyed.

In fashion it was an age of conformity too, a time when fashion strictly obeyed the dictates of Paris. *Vogue* commented, "The overall look was an overly sexual one; it was full of sharp outlines in breasts, narrow torso, sloping hips: aggressively female rather than softly feminine." The waist was small; the bust, emphasized and promoted by Hollywood, was large . . . the day of the "sweater girl." Foam rubber and plastic inserts increased the bosom size and raised and separated the breasts. Girdles were firm, their only concession to comfort being the increased lightness of their elastic fabrics. When Dior in 1954 decided that too much attention was being paid to the bustline and softened the look of his new line, newspaper stories insisted he had "abolished the bosom." "Not true," scorned the experts, and Carmel Snow, editor of *Harper's Bazaar* admonished that "a dropped bust which is not pushed up looks a horror."

Actually fashion was not keeping up with the times. Something far more important than the shape of the bosom or even of the Paris couture itself was happening—the coming of age of sportswear. The decade marked the beginning of the great migration from the city to the suburbs. Spurred by easy automobile access to the countryside, millions of middle-class whites left their old and dirty cities for the promise of green lawns, rolling hills, and quiet neighborhoods. From 1950 to 1955 the nation's population grew by some 14 million people, but 83 percent of this growth was in the suburbs. For the wealthy the cities were the place for formal, Paris-inspired, fashions; the countryside the place for the less expensive, informal, youth-inspired clothes. In the suburbs were the gardens, the golf courses, the tennis courts, the shopping centers, the swimming pools, the bowling alleys, the backyard barbecues, all demanding new, exciting, and comfortable clothes made specifically for the casual way of living.

The first years of the fifties were good to Warner's too. In spite of the failure of the company to practice the new science of marketing, sales increased an average of 14 percent a year, and share of market improved. The Warner's design department was undoubtedly the best in the industry. To keep up with the big swing to sportswear and the trend toward lighter and sheerer styles, we did our own experimenting with light fabrics at our mill in Canonchet, Rhode Island. Girdle blanks were knitted on the company's own circular knit machines and new yard goods were developed for even lighter styles. New power nets, of varying weights and strengths, were produced successfully on Wildman, Kay, and Kidde looms. All of these technical developments kept us design-wise ahead of our competitors.

While we kept our eye on sportswear, we continued to coordinate our styles with fashion. The Merry Widow and the Cinch were followed by such items as the "Five O'Clock" bra (the first bra to be worn as outerwear), eyelet bras to be seen under sheer blouses, and girdles and bras made in mauve, maroon, yellow, and red instead of just the traditional white and pink. For fashion's sake we turned out new padded and strapless bras, high top girdles for narrow waists, and panty girdles for the long waist effect.

When Dior in Paris exploded his bombshell about "abolishing the bra," our fashion director was in London. She flew to Paris and went to see Dior's collection herself, making notes and arrangements for pictures. Back home, she told us that the bosom had not "been abolished" but softened, while the waistline had been released and hips made tighter, thus producing what the fashion press was calling "the long line."

All this was significant for us because it meant a change in corsetry design. We also knew that much depended, not on the French designs themselves, but on what the American ready-to-wear designers adapted for the American market. Accordingly our two most experienced designers went into the New York workrooms of the top American designers, and created new Warner's styles alongside the new ready-to-wear. Within a month these new styles were sampled to our salesmen. By then more than thirty of the New York dress houses were using these Warner's styles to model their own new ready-to-wear based on Dior originals.

All this fashion excitement was stimulating and produced immediate sales but it did not result in improvement in our marketing skills. We needed more market penetration in our basics as well as our fashion styles, and this could be achieved only by coordination with the salesmen and the sales managers — and with my father. I tried to do part of the job myself, spending weeks on the road working with salesmen, visiting stores selling the merchandising of our line and our ads. It was a frustrating effort, especially with the difficulty of getting over the buyer's head to store management. In discussing plans for a sales conference in the spring of 1954, I was again emphasizing the need to sell the whole store, not just the buyer. I wrote my father "I do not think it would be enough just to show the new styles and the advertising to the salesmen. We must show them how Warner's can produce an improving profit for a store; they must become more familiar with mark-up and mark-down figures and turnover, with department location, the basic stocks, the stock control. The salesmen must learn to be merchandisers."

My father did not agree. He was pessimistic about the future, writing in 1952, "I am the only one of the company today who has any idea that this good business might not continue." Holding this belief at the beginning of one of the country's greatest boom periods, he ordered cuts in expenses, and refused to change the organization so that advertising and selling could work together. Rather he seemed to enjoy the competition between them.

In the ten year period between 1947 and 1956 Warner's sales had increased over 162 percent, almost triple the industry's increase of 55 percent. But beginning in 1954 the *rate* of increase dropped until 1956 showed only a modest improvement over the year before and 1957 an actual decrease. We started losing share of market.

The source of the problem was not hard to find. We were producing a large line of products for every age, figure type, and price line, while our most aggressive competitors were pin-pointing a market and exploiting it with specialty items and professional marketing skills. Technological developments in elastic materials which stretched comfortably around the body while giving reasonable control were making corset fitting unimportant and eliminating the need for so many different styles. One girdle or one bra would fit a higher percentage of the female population than before. The result was a rapid growth of competitors achieving substantial volume in one style or very few styles. If such a specialty brand, aimed at a large but specific segment of the market, was backed by heavy consumer advertising and astute marketing techniques, it could be devastating competition for a broad-based line like Warner's. Under such circumstances the products would sell through retail outlets with little help from corset buyers or corset fitters, only needing a working arrangement with store management and enough retail space, whether in the corset department or not, for their packaged products and their displays. Primary examples of this were Playtex and Maidenform. The former was spending more advertising money than Warner's on a few styles only, and the latter, a specialty house in lower-priced bras, was also outspending Warner's in advertising while concentrating on a limited number of bras alone. Both firms were growing faster than Warner's.

In view of these changes in the market place and in our competition, we were faced with the necessity of changing our whole way of doing business. No longer was it a matter of just coordinating the sales and advertising departments. Now the entire company would have to be brought under one umbrella to develop and pursue a new marketing strategy. Everybody would have to work together. Designing, production, production control, as well as advertising and sales, would all have to be part of one effort. If we did not do it, disaster threatened.

Yet at Warner's all departments were still going their separate ways with little coordination between them. The disagreement I had been having with my father over advertising and selling was really just a skirmish before the main battle between us. That main battle was to be over how the company would be organized and managed.

A thoughtful observer of Warner's in the LaRoche advertising agency, in a memo to me, observed, "Each Warner department is so jealous of the part it plays in the overall picture that any real coordination is impossible. The sales department attributes the lack of sales to inferior designing, poor deliveries, and mediocre advertising. Being notably poor

The Fifties

reporters, they are constantly requesting a new design based on a chance remark by a single buyer.

"The designing department is just as bad. They blame the lack of sales on poor quality production, poor deliveries, and weak selling. Like sales, they resent any criticism of their own effort. The production department must blame everybody other than their own inadequate production control and poor deliveries. The advertising department, in turn, attributes the problem to the lack of a coordinated effort and poor selling of their ideas. They will not admit that their advertising itself could be better."

What was needed was strong leadership to bring all these disparate units together. In 1957 my father was over seventy years old. He was taking increasingly long vacations; he was not available at crucial times; and yet he insisted that all departments continue to report directly to him and that he make all important decisions. He had been a successful manager in the thirties and forties when strict financial and expense controls were vital, but he was unable in the later fifties to understand what was happening in the market place. He wrote a general memo:

"You have heard me say many times that this is a sentimental business. I think we have had a tendency, under the influence of Playtex, to ignore the feelings of the buyers, the girls behind the counter, etc. We must make sure we appreciate the difference between our type of goods and Playtex's type of goods. Cheap merchandise lends itself to grocery and drug store types, all sorts of give-aways and gimmicks, packaging, etc, where our type of business is essentially a fitting story — a fitting story backed up by the good will of the people doing the selling.

"One of our greater weaknesses is that our customers think we have a case of 'swell head.' They have taken it upon themselves to level us out. Through talks and booklets on the operation of a corset department which the advertising department has been issuing, we have preached to the retailers, telling them how to run their businesses. Their reaction is 'Let them run their business, and we will run ours!' We must stop preaching to retailers and deal with the buyer first and foremost and go upstairs to management only when she will take us. Stop ignoring the buyer."

I was not alone in thinking that he was dead wrong. One experienced marketing man, outside the company, wrote, "It has been argued that the average corset buyer is a law unto herself. This is not an explanation for lost sales but rather an excuse. It is common practice to assume 'our business is different.' Why should a corset buyer be any different than a buyer of men's furnishings, or housewares, or photographic supplies? This argument is accepted as gospel by people who have never been in any other type of business and hardly seem qualified to make such a comparison."

An able young sales assistant reading our research reports on the success of Playtex noted, "The report shows up the weakness of basing our market strategy on the premise that their products and methods put them into a different kind of business. For each dozen they sell, there are one dozen less potential sales for us."

My father disregarded these critics, his solution to falling sales being the same as it had always been: cut costs. "In view of the drop in our sales for the first six months of 1957 and the prospects for the rest of the year, a cut of 10 percent in our expenses is the minimum for which we should settle. In order to save money, we must save people. We must cut out systems; we must cut out records; we must cut advertising. I know this ruling is going to cause consternation with our various managers, but it has to be done."

Fig Leaves and Fortunes

And it did cause consternation, especially coming at a time when our competitors were increasing, not decreasing, their marketing pressures and hence, their sales volumes.

John Field certainly could see how upset many of his managers were with his refusal to accept change. In the spring of 1957 he *did* make a concession: after ten years of urging he put both advertising and sales under me. His device for doing this was to make me president. Since L.T. Warner's death there had been no chairman of the board, my father serving as president, C.E.O., and acting chairman. He now proposed that he be elected chairman and C.E.O. and that I become president reporting to him. This move, rubber-stamped by the board, seemed at first glance helpful, but a closer look showed that little indeed was changed. I would be president in name only. True, I would have advertising and sales reporting to me, but *all other departments* would continue to report directly to him. Under this arrangement steps could be taken to coordinate advertising, promotion, and sales, but a true marketing strategy embracing all units of the company was still impossible.

Unless my father could be removed as C.E.O. (he showed no interest in retirement) such a strategy would remain out of the question.

My father was a complex, intense, austere man with little sense of humor. With the exception of L.T. Warner and his brother-in-law, Bradford G. Warner, who ran the Box Division, I never heard anybody at the company address him as "John"; it was always "Mr. Field." To those who unhesitantly accepted his opinions and his authority, he could be kind and generous, and to many employees in lower, middle, and even a few in top management, especially those who had struggled upward with him during the difficult days of the depression and the war, he was a paragon. To them, his opinion was the law. To those who questioned him, especially to those who had the effrontery to disagree with him, he presented a different face, harsh and non-forgiving.

For me, the situation was impossible. I was faced with two equally unattractive alternatives. I could go along with him, agreeing with him, not causing any trouble. This would put my personal relations, and my family's relations, with him on a friendly basis. But doing this, I was convinced, would result in a ruined company. Or I could fight to remove him and take control. Such a course would lead to a hopeless personal relationship. That is why any struggle for control of Warner Brothers loomed so unpleasant and so adversarial.

I talked it all over with my friends among the younger managers. Up until the war, because of his own ability and leadership, and because he did not have the money for high-priced associates, my father had by necessity surrounded himself largely with sycophants. As the company grew in the years after the war, he had had the foresight to hire a different kind of employees, younger, better educated, with minds and wills of their own. Now, along with me, these new employees were ready to question him. Together, we could clearly see the threats to the company, and hence to our own careers, that lay ahead. We could see that the old formula of simple frugality and caution would no longer work. We could see not only the rise of competition in the corset and bra business, but the dynamic changes taking place throughout the whole apparel industry. Large firms were replacing small, family-owned companies. Much of Warner's competition was now coming from major companies, often divisions of great corporations. We were alarmed by the resources, the advertising muscle, the sales coverage, the professional research, available to these new competitors which were allowing them to become, for the first time in the apparel industry, true consumer marketers. We could also see how stores and store chains were getting

The Fifties

bigger too, building a concentration of retail power in fewer and fewer hands. Large manufacturers could command the attention of these large retailers; small manufacturers, especially those concentrating on only one product for one small department, could not. The day of relying on the department store buyer was disappearing as his or her influence in the retail world evaporated, replaced by planning and programming between manufacturer and retailer.

Looking even farther ahead, we could see even a bigger challenge. Because the Warner Brothers Company was virtually a one-product organization, it was in danger of becoming obsolete. The vagaries of fashion or technological change could destroy the whole girdle and bra business (within a few years the girdle business *did* virtually disappear). Safety, it seemed, lay in a variety of products, not all of which would go out of favor. Men, women, and children would wear *something*. Shouldn't we know what that was and be prepared to market it?

At his age John Field was simply not equipped by experience or interest to lead Warner's into this strange new world. We were not disloyal to him personally; to a greater or lesser degree all of us were fond of him; certainly all of us respected his accomplishments, knowing that without him there would have been no Warner Brothers for us to inherit.

So we made our decision. It was time for a change. Together we would fight for control of the company.

In the last days of 1957 and the first months of 1958 we plotted our course. The decision on who was to run the company would be made by the board of directors. This board was divided into members of the Warner family, most of them not active in the business, plus a group of younger employees now in charge of operations. This group consisted of men like Cameron Clark, and E. John Van Ort, who were soon to be managers of the Box Division, Henry Coogan and H. Sumner Farwell, who ran corset design and production respectively, Bradford N. Warner, a young member of the Warner family who was involved with company public relations, and myself. All of us could be counted on to vote for change. My father, though married to a member of the Warner family, owned little of the common stock, which over the years had become widely dispersed. He had only one vote on the board and could influence, but not control, others. The Warner family board members were largely concerned with company earnings and dividends, on which they depended for their incomes. While they recognized their obligations to my father for all he had done for the company and for them, they would vote for whom they thought would make the most money in the future.

Even from the perspective of thirty years later, it is still difficult to write objectively about the fervid discussions and arguments of the early months of 1958. Certainly it was an emotional time, especially for me and, I am sure, for my father. He did not give up easily. To the senior Warner directors he painted a dire picture of what would happen "if these radical young men are given control." We would "go haywire," and expenses "would go crazy." Sales and earnings would collapse while money was squandered in hasty ventures. For our part we painted an equally dismal picture of the future with an aging John Field still in charge: Warner's falling farther and farther behind competition, a one-product company stagnating without plans and marketing skills. Then we advanced an arrogant threat: if we were not given the authority to run the company, all of us would resign en masse.

Fig Leaves and Fortunes

That probably won the day for us. Even those members of the board most loyal to my father were concerned about the future of a company headed by a seventy-three year-old man and a completely new and unproven executive team. He said he could, and would, create such a team without any of us, but most members of the board were reluctant to take the chance.

The first weekend in March 1958 John Field played his last card. To his home on Sunday he summoned most members of the Warner family who were on the board and any other board members he thought loyal to him. He repeated his charges of inexperience and irresponsibility on our part, that while he was prepared to build a new organization, he did not believe that most of us would carry out our threats to resign. Probably I would have to go, and would go, but he was sure Coogan, Farwell and the rest would stay, and he was prepared to give them more authority to run the company with himself merely an advisor.

The group was sympathetic to him; they were his friends. They wished it had not come to this. But later that week, my father lost the battle. By the simple device of shifting the "authority and responsibility" for running the company from the chairman to the president, they voted to end John Field's long tenure as chief executive officer. The vote was unanimous, with John Field himself joining in to vote "yes."

10

Into the Sixties

*T*HE ORDERED world of the fifties was turned upside down as the sixties began. It was to be the decade of Kennedy's election and assassination. It was the decade of the Bay of Pigs, the Berlin Wall, of the Cuban missile crisis, of Lyndon Johnson and Vietnam, of civil rights demonstrators, and ghetto riots, of campus upheavals, of the murders of Bob Kennedy and Martin Luther King, of the hippies and drop-outs, of the pill, drugs, violent crime, Woodstock, of the riotous 1968 Democratic convention, of Nixon's return, and the landing on the moon.

The world of fashion was equally chaotic. The couture designers, French, American, Italian, British, lost their position as fashion arbiters, displaced by the young of every nation. In the early days of the decade the fashions, influenced by Jacqueline Kennedy, were conservative and gentle. Millions of women imitated her pillbox hat, skirt just below the knees, waistless sheath, shoes with pointed toes and slender heels. But as the decade wore on and the established world came unglued, fashion came unglued with it. In London Mary Quant started the miniskirt fad, and skirts crept higher and higher until they reached microskirt length. "Don't trust anybody over thirty," commanded the young and wore blue jeans, beads, and long hair. "I watch what the kids are putting together for themselves," admitted Rudi Gernreitch, the designer, "then I formalize it, give it something of my own, perhaps, and that is fashion."

"Burn the bra," ordered the feminists, but fortunately for Warner's not too many women obeyed the command. Girdles, bras, and lingerie *did*, however, grow lighter and briefer. The padded bras and firm girdles of the fifties disappeared, replaced by natural curves. Clothes that were decollete, very short, sometimes transparent, required body stockings or pantyhose, or, for the daring, nothing at all. There were matching sets of bras and bikini briefs in nylon lace, the bras themselves mere wisps of cloth mounted on elastic straps. "Drive, jump, ride, stretch, accelerate into spring with briefer, simpler foundations you can put on and forget," suggested *Vogue*.

In such a wild fashion climate the future of a small foundation garment manufacturer was perilous indeed. Would women continue to wear any bras and girdles at all? It seemed to us, newly in charge of our own destiny, that diversification into other products was a vital necessity for survival.

But first we had to put our own house in order. Because we had thought so much about what we would do if we had the authority, it did not take long to draw up a plan:

We would restrict the sale of Warner's to those upscale department and specialty stores who would understand, and appreciate, our design leadership and quality products. If this meant temporary loss of volume, so be it.

As a result, our prices would be above average.

Our production costs would be lowered through location of plants in low-cost areas (particularly the south, Mexico, and the Caribbean) and through high efficiency in those plants with innovative mechanization.

We would maintain our design department as the best in the business.

Most important, we would adopt modern marketing. Gone would be the long lines with too many styles. Instead we would present sharply focused lines with a few, highly promotable items appealing to a targeted market. We would become experts at moving our products *through*, not just *into*, stores, so that Warner's would become the most profitable intimate apparel line for the nation's retailers.

Because the growth of large chain stores was greater than that of department and specialty stores, and because many of our own stores wanted their own private label goods, we would organize a unit separate from the Warner's brand to design and produce girdles and bras for sale under our customers' own names.

The first chance we had to discuss all this with the salesmen was at the national sales conference in November of 1958 at Ponte Vedra, Florida. It was a dismal time. Total sales for the year were off 9 percent, profits off 28 percent. In retrospect, however, this conference turned out to be the turning point. Now we could direct the salesmen the way they should have been directed for many previous years. They were told that we expected them to become business partners with their customers. Those who could not, or would not, had no future with Warner's.

Five years later, in 1963, we went back to Ponte Vedra for another sales conference. This time the mood was ebullient: Warner's was on its way to a record year in sales and profits. The salesmen were congratulated on having learned the fundamentals of planning, partnership, and service. I told them, "In 1958, when we were last here, Warner's as a company sold $27,431,000 in merchandise. Last year we sold $50,952,000. This year we will sell between $55 and $60 million. Next year we will sell better than $80 million, and within a very short time we will top $100 million."

It was not done solely by Warner's; much of the additional volume came from diversification. Actually, in a small way, the Warner Brothers Company had been a diversified enterprise for many years. Back in 1890 the doctors Warner, always alert to saving a dollar, began producing their own boxes for packing, storing, and shipping their corsets. Box machinery was virtually unknown at the time, and those early functional set-up boxes were cut and assembled by hand. Other local firms, notably Holmes and Edwards in silverware and Yale and Towne in hardware, began buying their boxes from Warner's, and during World War I the demand for Warner's boxes was so great that branch plants were

Into the Sixties

set up in Stamford, Danbury, Stratford, and Torrington. By 1920 the sales of the box division had reached $1.6 million.

The decade of the twenties was as disastrous for Warner's Box as it was for Warner's corsets. Rapid changes were taking place in point-of-sale displays and promotions, and with these changes came modern packaging. The box became a sales tool. Unfortunately, with the losses in its dominant corset business, Warner's did not have the money to purchase the new folding box and color presses just coming on the market. By the end of the decade the volume of the box business had slipped to a mere $300,000 with results in red ink, and the very existence of the division in doubt.

But the company had the courage to stick with the box division, and in the early thirties John Field assigned the task of rebuilding the business to his brother-in-law, Bradford G. Warner, grandson of one of the founders, and son of D.H. Warner. Gradually, as corset sales and profits regained their momentum, money became available for box-building equipment, and printing, die-cutting, and folding presses were purchased. World War II accelerated demand as Bridgeport neighbors like General Electric and Remington Arms bought huge quantities of boxes for their war goods.

By the end of the war the box division was clearly two separate businesses: folding boxes for volume orders and set-up boxes for highly-styled packaging for cosmetic firms and others where the cost of the box was incidental to its customer appeal. Display boxes for customers such as Prince Matchabelli, Elizabeth Arden, Chanel, Vicks, Revlon, and Remington shavers were all made by Warner's, and by the end of the forties, demand was so great that a new building of 90,000 sq. ft. was constructed to house the folding box department alone.

But troubles came to the box business in the late fifties just as they had for Warner's girdles and bras. The most serious problem lay with the cheaper volume sales where Warner's could not compete on a tonnage basis with companies that owned their own board mills. These integrated firms, taking only one profit on their mill and their packaging, could shave their prices far below Warner's.

A change in strategic thinking was needed to plan the future, and our new management acted quickly. We appointed Cameron Clark, Jr. as manager of the box division, replacing his father-in-law, Bradford G. Warner. Cameron had come to us several years before from General Electric and had served his apprenticeship in all departments of box. He now drew up a strategic plan whose essence was for Warner's to concentrate on the small volume, high quality end of the packaging spectrum, leaving the volume business to others. Within this selected niche, we would provide a complete packaging service for our customers, embracing not only production of boxes, but research and design services as well. Like its associate in apparel, Warner's box would try to become the fashion leader in its field, thus justifying its higher prices. To dramatize the change in strategy the name of the division was changed from the Box division to the Packaging division.

Even though both our girdle and bra business and packaging were now on a profitable course, further diversification was still necessary for the Warner Brothers Company. The turbulent conditions developing in the fashion industry made this doubly important. As mentioned before, we were a small, mostly one-product business, still basically family-owned, in a volatile and changing industry, without the size and accompanying muscle to command large retailer attention. Particularly vulnerable were our stockholders, two hundred sixty-six of them at that time, mostly third and fourth generation descendants of the company founders, plus current and former Warner's employees who over the years had purchased or been given shares of stock. These people, most of them not wealthy, depended on Warner's dividends for a substantial share of their income. A speculative stock like the Warner Brothers Company was not their safest investment. Many of them were getting older and needed an assured market for their stock to avoid inheritance valuation problems. Their children, no longer employed by, nor even interested in, Warner's, wanted a market into which they could sell their stock.

Just as the sixties began, we submitted our recommendation to the board. This has become a memorable document in the history of the Warner Brothers Company, proposing a dramatic change in its corporate structure. The report outlined the current situation and suggested there were three possible directions for the company to take:

Alternative 1) Continue as an independent company solely in our types of foundation garments and in the box business.

Alternative 2) Become part of a larger organization (sell out), exchanging Warner's stock for the stock of a larger company, presumably listed on a stock exchange.

Alternative 3) Become a large, publicly-owned, diversified firm ourselves through expansion in the foundation garment and box businesses and into related products.

Alternative 1 was the easiest, but did not solve any of our long-range problems. Alternative 2 solved all the problems but was not a solution favored by management or the major Warner's stockholders, who did not want to lose control of the company. It was, however, the course recommended by our bankers and financial advisers as least risky. Alternative 3 was the most difficult but also most full of potential rewards. This was the course management preferred.

After much deliberation and to our vast relief, the Warner's directors agreed with management, authorizing us to proceed with a program of:

1) Expansion within the corset and box industries and diversification into related products and industries.

2) Establishment of a public market for the company stock.

Now the task was to research a whole range of possibilities and to draw up a specific program. It was only logical for us to concentrate on the apparel industry, which was really the only business we knew well, and on those areas of apparel where there were strong brand names and a degree of stability against fashion change — also where there were growth opportunities in accord with anticipated changes in consumer preferences and life styles. Within these apparel areas we would search out companies with existing management strength, a reputation for quality, creativity, and integrity, a strong brand name (preferably one or two in a market niche), and good standing with existing Warner's retail customers.

These studies pointed to three markets:

1) Intimate apparel.

2) Menswear accessories, particularly men's shirts.

3) Men's and women's sportswear.

The company already had a strong position in intimate apparel, but it needed to increase its ability to develop new products, particularly in stretch materials, both knitted and woven. It had to broaden its distribution into the large chain stores like Sears, Wards, and Penneys and to offer coordination with, and production of, lingerie, which was drawing ever closer to girdles and bras in design, color, and selling.

Outside of intimate apparel, men's shirts was a promising field because, like girdles and bras, it was largely a reorder business with quality in construction, materials, and basic styling more significant than fashion innovation. Most important of all was sportswear. Sooner or later the extreme fashions of the sixties would disappear as all extreme fashions in history have (where was the bustle?), but American living habits were changing rapidly and permanently. Formality was out; casual living was in. Any apparel company not deeply involved in sportswear would only be a loser.

Within these three fields we started our search for specific opportunities. Intimate apparel was first. In July of 1960 we purchased a supplier of ours, Dawn Fabrics of Westerly, Rhode Island, a manufacturer of elastic-woven fabrics. As we had promised in our original strategic plan, we launched a new subsidiary, Exclusive Apparel, to design and manufacture intimate apparel for large chain stores, sold under the store name. Girdle and bra distribution was increased abroad where we purchased our former licensees in Canada, France, Belgium, and Germany and built new plants in Northern Ireland and Belgium. To achieve lower production costs, sewing plants were opened in Mexico, Costa Rica, and Guatamala. Finally, we fulfilled our requirement for lingerie facilities in September of 1960 by purchasing the Laros Company of Bethlehem, Pennsylvania, a medium-sized producer of daywear and sleepwear, whose list of retail customers paralled those of Warner's.

None of these moves, however, concentrated as they were in intimate apparel, was major enough to give us real product diversification. Other steps were necessary, and one giant step came quickly. In November we bought all the assets of the C.F. Hathaway Company of Waterville, Maine, for $3,500,000 in cash. America's oldest manufacturer of men's shirts and its largest producer of high-priced, quality shirts, Hathaway was one of the best known brands in the entire apparel industry. Millions of people were familiar with its famous "Man with the Eye Patch" advertising campaign. It also operated a Lady Hathaway division, which had the potential to give us a small, but promising, foothold in the expanding women's sportswear field.

It is highly unlikely that Charles Foster Hathaway of Plymouth, Massachusetts, ever met George Bryan Brummel, "Beau Brommel" to his friends, of London, England. Yet in the first half of the nineteenth century they were both engaged in trying to make their male contemporaries dress more fashionably. Beau Brommel was an English dandy, one of a small coterie of haughty Englishmen whose prime purpose in life was to vaunt their highly eclectic tastes in literature, living, and especially in gentlemen's fashions. The Prince of Wales is said to have spent hours watching Beau Brommel dress in order to fathom the secret of his impeccable taste.

Charles Hathaway, impoverished descendant of Nicholas Hathaway who had landed at Plymouth in 1630, was the second in a family of ten children. He had little, or no, education and went to work in a nail factory at the age of eleven and at fifteen became a printer with the publishers of *Webster's Dictionary*. By some twist of fate, however, like Beau Brommel he had a flair for fashion, for elegance, for taste. At about the same time that Brommel in England was introducing the idea of starching men's collars, thus making them stiffer and higher, Hathaway was designing elegant men's shirts replete with frills and ruffles for American gentlemen.

Fig Leaves and Fortunes

Charles Foster Hathaway, part-time Baptist preacher and founder of the Hathaway Shirt Company.

In 1837 Hathaway began making shirts in the parlor of his own home on Appleton Street in Waterville, Maine. He had tried making shirts in Plymouth and in Boston, but found "sweatshop conditions" unbearable. In Waterville he found conditions more to his liking. There his workers came into town from the surrounding farms for a week of sewing or ironing and returned home for the Sabbath. At the beginning of each working day, Mr. Hathaway would lead them all in hymn and prayer.

As can be seen from this daily routine, Mr. Hathaway was also a sometime Baptist preacher, and the conflict between his heavenly and worldly interests tormented him all his life. To his wife, Temperance, he wrote in 1840, the year of their marriage, "My constant attendance to wordly concerns retards my soul in its progress toward heaven."

Mr. Hathaway's progress toward heaven was conceivably also retarded by the fact that he was an extremely irascible and cantankerous husband, employer, and parishioner. He refused to permit Temperance to wear buttons on her clothes. Everything had to be fastened by hooks and eyes because buttons were too ornamental. He was in constant disagreement with his employees over wages, with his partners over finances, and with his various pastors over matters pertaining to God. In the midst of one such church argument he wrote that the pastor "made me out a liar and a hypocrite. Therefore I would not trouble him by my further presence at his communion table." Once he wrote another pastor, Dr. E.H. Burrage, that he had lost respect for Dr. Burrage's faithfulness and integrity, and that therefore he intended to leave the Baptist Church and start his own church.

In spite of himself Mr. Hathaway seems to have succeeded in the shirt business. In those days the sewing machine had not yet been invented, and shirt production was entirely by

Into the Sixties

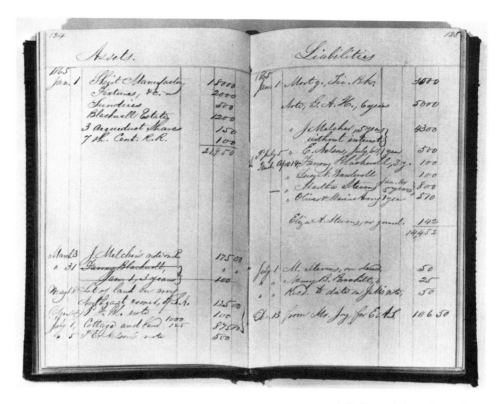

A Hathaway balance sheet of 1865.

hand, in Mr. Hathaway's case being limited to two dozen a week. Every two or three months he would travel by stage coach to Boston, personally carrying his shirts, to sell them to a men's furnishing store he owned there and gradually to other stores. It is interesting to note that because of the elaborate frills and ruffles of those yesterday garments, the ironing was more difficult and crucial than the sewing, and the standard output of an ironer was only one shirt per day. The weekly rate in Mr. Hathaway's parlor was $1.50 to $2.00 for sewers, and $3.00 to $5.50 for ironers.

Sales appear to have increased enough for Mr. Hathaway so that in 1853 he could purchase an acre of land on Appleton Street for the site of a new Hathaway shirt factory, where it was to be located for over 100 years. It was there too, just before the Civil War, that his first sewing machines were bought and put into operation, and it was there that shirts were made for the Union army. By 1872, still two years before the Doctors Warner founded their enterprise, Mr. Hathaway's journal reported $58,000 in assets. At the time of his death in 1893 those assets had risen to over $100,000, all of which he left to the Baptist Missionary Society. By that time he seems to have been welcomed back into the Baptist Church.

There is evidence also that before he died he was able to reconcile his avarice with his sanctity. In this, Temperance seems to have been a great help. She was not always sympathetic when he complained about the church and the pastor, saying, with tears, that "it seemed wrong to say so much of faults and nothing of virtue." Before his death he commented, "These words led me to see how strongly this had always been my character so

Fig Leaves and Fortunes

as to spoil my influence and make me dreaded and shunned. I trust the lesson, though so late, is the best one of my life."

Obviously the Missionary Society could not operate the shirt business so it was sold to Clarence A. Leighton, an enterprising salesmen for Hathaway, who in addition to shirts carried a line of lace-trimmed pantaloons and a line of American flags. Colonel Leighton, as he was called, prospered in the shirt business to a far greater degree than had Mr. Hathaway, possibly, as one of his biographers has opined, because he was "more of a salesman and less of a minister." In any case, he was very much alive to the fashion changes of his day and adapted his shirt designs accordingly. Under his guidance the frills and ruffles of the Hathaway line disappeared to be replaced by the new full-length starched bosom and cuff shirts of the early 1900s.

In 1915 Colonel Leighton died and his son Edward (Ned) took over Hathaway with general manager, Frank Smith, who had started under Charles Hathaway years before. Under their leadership the plant on Appleton Street reached a weekly production of seven hundred dozen shirts, even though flow-through was hampered by constant style changes. The long, stiff bosom got shorter and narrower and finally disappeared. It was replaced by the first completely soft shirt with a starched neckband to which the stiff collar of the day was attached. From about 1915 there was a sudden switch to colored shirts, so much so that the white shirt almost vanished during the early 1920s except for evening wear.

What men *really* wanted was a shirt with a collar attached. During World War I Hathaway made many of these simple shirts for the soldiers, and the men returning home remembered how comfortable they were. When it came to high-class shirts, such as Hathaway's regular styles, however, the problem with the collar-attached shirt was the habit of the collar points turning up, or curling. This was true whether they were fully-starched collars, soft collars, or fused collars. Hathaway partially solved the problem by putting a removable celluloid strip down the front inside edge of the collar, and, if this was still not entirely satisfactory, by providing a collar pin which held the points together. It was not until some years later that the bi-angle collar stay, also invented by Hathaway, put an end to the problem.

As in the case of Warner's, the twenties and early thirties brought troubles to Hathaway. Total volume slipped from $600,000 to $125,000. Ned Leighton was discouraged and prepared to abandon his business. Suddenly, however, there appeared saviors in the form of a man named Ellerton Jette and his partner, Charles McCarthy. Both of them had been salesmen for the Buffalo Shirt Company and, anxious to get into their own business, they saw potential in the Hathaway name and reputation. They offered to take the business off Leighton's hands, paying him little, but assuming all his debts and risks. Of the two partners McCarthy seems to have been the better businessman, while Jette was the more flamboyant with a flair for fashion, color, design, and salesmanship. Jette had fun at whatever he was doing, even though he was perhaps too enthusiastic, too optimistic, too self-confident, to be a reliable profit maker. His ideas, however, stimulated the men's shirt market for many years and made Hathaway its fashion leader.

It was Jette, along with his designer, Ashley Logan, who in 1937 made the seemingly obvious discovery that a man's neck was not round but oval, and that necks pitched forward from the shoulder and not straight up in the air. This discovery led to the design of a new collar that fitted the natural contours of the neck. It was Jette too, a year later, who insisted that all Hathaway shirts be made only by single-needle construction similar to

Into the Sixties

Charles McCarthy and Ellerton Jette, owners of Hathaway in the early 1930s.

that used in the most expensive custom shirts. This process required double sewing time, twice the number of operators, and increased cost by 60 percent, but in Jette's opinion made a far superior product. Other Jette innovations included the previously mentioned bi-angle collar stay, sleeves made of a single piece of cloth, square cornered cuffs, and the three-hole button which was stronger and better looking than the conventional four-hole button, but as in most of Jette's ideas, costlier to make. It was Jette too, an enthusiastic and inveterate traveler, who searched the world for exotic fabrics, bringing back madras and silks from India, ginghams from Scotland, prints from France, broadcloth from Japan, and Viyella from England. It was Jette too, who, with a flair for the picturesque, bought Hathaway House in New York City, a lovely old brick townhouse in the Murray Hill section, which served as sales headquarters for Hathaway as well as Jette's New York home. To decorate Hathaway House he hung the sales offices and his living quarters with the primitive American paintings he had been collecting for years from New England farms and which made him an important figure in the art world. In 1956 he and Mrs. Jette, who before their marriage had been an antique buyer for Lord and Taylor, gave their American Heritage Collection to the Colby College (Maine) Museum of Art. Later they also gave their collection of works of American artists of the Impressionist Period to Colby.

It was Ellerton Jette too, as the story goes, who was sitting in the first-class lounge of the ocean liner, *Queen Mary*, with a young advertising man named David Ogilvy when Lewis Douglas, the American Ambassador to the Court of St. James, entered. Mr. Douglas wore a patch over one eye. Both Jette and Ogilvy noted that all eyes in the room turned instinctively to the man wearing an eye patch, and in that second a great advertising idea

Fig Leaves and Fortunes

The famous Hathaway "Man with the Eyepatch"
was Baron George Wrangall.

was born. For many years thereafter the model wearing the Hathaway shirt in the company's magazine advertisements wore an eye patch. When Hathaway was purchased by Warner's, *Newsweek* magazine hailed the "marriage of the Merry Widow to the Man with the Eye Patch."

Jette was always an elitist and insisted on the exactly correct model with the exactly correct aristocratic lineage for the Hathaway Man. David Ogilvy, perhaps even more elitist, found that correct man for him. He was Baron George Wrangall who had been born in 1903 in Orlina, Russia, on the estate of his uncle, Count Nicholas Stragonoff. His mother was the daughter of the Knight of Malta and of Duchess Lillie, lady-in-waiting to the Empress. His father was Captain Peter Baron Wrangall of the Imperial Russian Navy, one of the fourteen senators who freed the serfs under Emperor Alexander II. During the Bolshevik Revolution Baron Wrangall fled Russia for America, where, when Ogilvy discovered him, he was a society editor for a New York newspaper. He was handsome, charming, had impeccable manners and a marvelously debonair way with both men and women. He was perfect for Jette and Hathaway.

It was inevitable, probably, that Ellerton Jette's extravagance would lead Hathaway into financial trouble. When Charles McCarthy died, his restraining influence died with him, and Jette went on a spending spree. The company had already greatly expanded production facilities since the war, in 1945 opening a second plant in Waterville and in 1950 adding 100,000 sq.ft. of factory space in Lowell, Massachusetts. Now in 1956 Jette purchased the "Number Two Lockwood Cotton Mill" from Deering Milliken in Waterville and spent almost a million dollars in remodeling it. The old building was stripped down to its walls and foundation, the brick walls inside and out sand-blasted, pointed up, and left in natural color. All the multi-plane windows and sashes were replaced by modern windows. New

Into the Sixties

piping, plumbing, heating, and complete boiler rooms were installed, as well as a sprinkler system and fluorescent lighting. The beautiful hardwood floor which replaced the building's ancient wide planking would have been a credit to the most lordly mansion, as would the lovely primitive paintings from Jette's own collection which adorned the office. Mrs. Jette, who had not only worked as an antique buyer but was also a trained interior decorator, was responsible for the color scheme — brick red on woodwork and window frames, light pastel blue to delicate aquamarines in both sewing rooms and offices. It was, very possibly, the most elegant factory building in America. It was also one of the most expensive.

But Jette was not yet finished. He now bought the Gantner swimsuit company in California with the idea of diversifying into a different apparel market, and then the Wellington Hathaway Company, the Canadian distributor of Hathaway shirts. Both ventures were unsuccessful and soon liquidated, Gantner in 1958 with a loss of $822,000 and Wellington in 1959 with losses of $175,000. While all this was going on, Jette made several trips abroad and to India, where, enamored of the beautiful colors of India madras (the ads read "guaranteed to fade"), he bought thousands of yards to be made into shirts for the American market. They received fashion acclaim, but sold poorly. Jette was stuck with a huge inventory.

The result of these extravagances was that Hathaway lost $1,562,398 in 1958 and narrowly escaped bankruptcy as the banks, from whom the company had borrowed money, stepped in to restore order. At their insistence Jette was moved up to the position of chairman, while Vincent J. McDermott, the treasurer, was made president and C.E.O. In this capacity Jette could still design and sell shirts, while McDermott and the banks controlled his finances. The strategy worked, and by 1960 progress had been made in restoring Hathaway to profitability. While sales had dropped from $13,151,914 in 1958 to $9,903,327 in the year ending January 30, 1960, financial results had improved from the disastrous loss of 1958 to a respectable profit of $612,889. This was enough of a favorable upturn to make the company highly saleable, and it *was* sold in early 1960 to an investment group headed by Samuel J. Holtzman, an officer of the Baltimore Luggage Company. The syndicate also included A.M. Sonnabend, chairman of Botany Industries and president of the Hotel Corporation of America. It was from this group that Warner's purchased Hathaway later that year. Holtzman, Sonnabend, and their friends made substantial profits on the deal.

In retrospect, we at Warner's purchased Hathaway at an opportune time when its profits, and hence its price, were still low, but when its future was promising. In the years after that, Hathaway was rarely a disappointment. Perhaps because it was our first major diversification, it remained our favorite acquisition. We were correct in seeing in the company of the "Man with the Eye Patch" the same opportunity which Ellerton Jette and Charles McCarthy had seen in it twenty-eight years earlier.

So 1960, a momentous year for the Warner Brothers Company, ended. It was the second year under our new management, and the first when the road to the future became clear. We had strengthened our Warner's division, purchased several of our foreign licensees, established a packaging service, got a start in lingerie, and bought Hathaway. In the annual report for that year we described our strategy. "In the future, as in the past, we expect the bulk of the company's business to be derived from branded merchandise. Each year it grows more difficult and costly to establish new brands. Thus it was no accident that in our first moves to diversify, our company sought out and acquired a quality brand of wide acceptance. In any further expansion, our intention would be to acquire brands of comparable character. This is the soundest possible long-term strategy for protecting and expanding the size, security, competitive position, and profitability of the Warner Brothers Company."

Into the Sixties

11

The Late Sixties

LL THIS HAPPENED in 1960, and yet 1960 was only the *first* year of the sixties. True, John F. Kennedy, heralding a new generation of young leaders, had been elected president but the political and social turmoil of the decade still lay ahead.

It was in the sixties that sportswear first swept the fashion world. Destined to be far more permanent than the ephemeral fashion oddities of the decade, it became America's first major contribution to the wardrobes of men, women, and children everywhere. Designers like Bill Blass, Bonnie Cashin, Perry Ellis, Anne Klein, and later, Calvin Klein made American-designed sportswear known and worn throughout the world.

Characteristic of sportswear was its youthful lightness in fabric and construction, requiring new lightness in undergarments as well. *Vogue* commented that "the new lightness of clothes was not only aesthetic, nor merely a result of fashion's newly acquired youth: a new group of fibres had actually reduced lingerie weight." *Vogue* was referring to the introduction in 1960 of a yarn called Lycra*, developed by DuPont, with which Warner's, along with other companies, had been experimenting for a number of years. This new fibre was not only sheerer than rubber, it was also superior in strength, dyability, elasticity, and flex life. In its own mills Warner's had developed an uncovered Lycra which was even sheerer than ordinary Lycra, and much lighter than any other elastic fibre. For the lighter and briefer under fashions which sportswear in the sixties was going to require, uncovered Lycra was exactly the right thing. Even the names of styles introduced by Warner's — "Birthday Suit," "Little Godiva," "Stretch-bra," indicate the direction in which fashion was moving and the trend toward ever lighter elastic materials.

"I've worked here all my life," a bitter John Field wrote me in August 1960, "and I've always figured that Warner Brothers, in view of what I have done for them, would carry

*A registered trademark of DuPont.

Warner's answer to the sportswear boom of the 1960s was the Stretch-bra using stretch lace.

me the rest of my life on the regular salary I have been receiving. This is a precedent set up in the case of Mr. D.H. Warner and Mr. L.T. Warner, but apparently this is not to be the case. Events have so developed that my income will be cut 50 percent.

"When I was made president in the very early 30s, Warner Brothers was selling about $3 million. When I moved out as president, the sales were $30 million. Warner Brothers in the early 30s was busted. In 1932 my salary was $20,000. In the next few years my salary was cut along with everyone else. I earned $17,000 in '33, $17,600 in '34, and $20,000 in '34. In '39 I got up as high as $37,000.

"During all these years I was never given an opportunity to acquire any stock. At one time I asked about buying company stock which had a book value about $10.00. I was offered it at $25.00 per share! Naturally I did not buy any.

"I not only developed the sales and profits of the company, but also developed the organization you have today.

"At the time I took on this job, I was advised by friends that I was foolish to stay here. I was offered two jobs outside, paying me a good salary and a good opportunity. I was too loyal for my own good. I figured I had married into the Warner family, and my obligation was to them. I stayed, took on the job, and earned millions for everybody but myself."

When I received that letter, I should have taken warning. He was wrong in some respects. Contrary to what he said, the board was treating him kindly, keeping him as chairman for ten years after his retirement from active management, not cutting his salary 50 percent but instead for five years paying him a salary higher than mine as C.E.O. (1964 figures: John Field $94,600, John W. Field $90,700) and a substantial stipend after that for doing very little.

The Late Sixties

Warner's is listed on the New York Stock Exchange February 4, 1963. John Field is at the far left; the author third from left.

But he was right too in saying that he was "foolish" to have stayed to manage a company in which he had little ownership. He had not become a wealthy man even though he had saved the Warner Brothers Company and the Warner family from bankruptcy. He never became the large stockholder he deserved to be. He should have learned from his father-in-law, D.H. Warner, who vowed never to be involved in the management of a company unless he was a substantial owner.

Unfortunately, I myself was about to make the same mistake. I was building a company in which I was only a small stockholder, not an owner. Looking to the future, this meant that, like my father, I would have little control over the ultimate destiny of the company, and if the company was successful, millions of dollars would be made, but not by me.

The moment when Warner Brothers became a public company in 1961 was the time I should have acted. All acquisitions up to that time, including Laros and Hathaway, had been made for cash, and we now owed the banks $6,500,000 on short-term notes. This was certainly not troublesome because our *current* assets were three times that amount, but we could not afford to buy major sportswear companies by simply paying cash through borrowed money. Accordingly in May of 1961 we sold 200,000 shares of new common stock through Lehman Brothers for $15 per share. In this way we established a public market for our stock and created a currency which could be used for acquisitions without impairing our financial strength. At the same time our large stockholders acquired a liquid market for valuing or selling their stock. Two years later we went on the New York Stock Exchange.

In retrospect, that was the time I should have insisted that, if I was going to manage the company into the future, I should have had an opportunity to earn, or be given, a substantial block of voting stock. I did not do so.

Fig Leaves and Fortunes

We now turned our attention to sportswear which was becoming ever more important as the movement to suburbia accelerated. True, we held a tenuous position in sportswear with Lady Hathaway and with the sport shirts of men's Hathaway but they were unimportant to the stores. We were noticing that whenever our Hathaway salesmen attempted to sell our men's knit sport shirts or sweaters, our products were adversely compared to those of a brand named Puritan. Our investigation of Puritan showed it to be the descendant of the old Puritan Knitting Mills of Altoona, Pennsylvania, owned largely by the Frank Titelman family, and that it had an outstanding and growing reputation in casual sportswear for men.

The company had been founded in Philadelphia in 1909 by I.S. Titelman, who at that time operated a small business making men's trousers. It so happened that a neighbor of Mr. Titelman owned a financially hard-pressed knitting operation, whose equipment became available at little cost. Mr. Titelman decided to buy the machinery and start knitting sweaters. After all, he reasoned, pants and sweaters went together. They were simple, functional, and had a similar market peak: the fall and winter. He could take orders a year in advance, then produce away for a full twelve months.

Puritan Knitting Mills, as Mr. Titelman called his enterprise, was a modest success through the years of World War I and the twenties. Mr. Titelman's four sons joined the business, notably Frank Titelman in 1917, who eventually acquired control from his brothers. The same depression of the thirties, which almost destroyed Warner's and Hathaway, made itself felt at Puritan, perhaps in an even more acute form. Not only did the market for sweaters deteriorate, but the textile industry in the Philadelphia area was hit hard by sudden and serious labor unrest. In 1934, Frank Titelman, unable to continue to operate in Philadelphia, moved his business to Altoona, Pennsylvania, where adequate labor was available. The giant Pennsylvania Railroad shops were laying off workers, as was a large silk mill, which was reeling, not only under the impact of the depression, but also through the advent of synthetic fibres.

In Altoona Frank Titelman's beginnings were slow and deliberate. He started with 58 employees in 20,000 sq.ft. of the abandoned silk mill. But his progress was rapid, and within a short time he occupied the full 220,000 sq. ft. of the building. In 1938 he added woven sportswear to his line, and two years later sport shirts and swim trunks. During World War II Puritan manufactured some 2.5 million army fatigue jackets and more than a million high-neck sweaters for U.S. troops.

By 1955 the company, now operated by Frank and his son, Richard, had a sales volume of $7 million and employed 700 workers. In that year a bold decision was made to invest in equipment for knitting sport shirts and sweaters on full-fashioned machines. Thus Puritan became one of the first U.S. knitters to major in this rapidly growing knitting technology. The move proved highly successful, and by 1959 annual sales had reached $13 million, and the company had installed a dye house and laundry for control over the color and finish of its products. In 1963, when the Titelmans were approached by Warner's, they had a company doing $25 million a year, employing 1,800 workers, with a new 140,000 sq. ft. office and shipping facility, and most important, a profit of over half a million dollars.

Beginning in the late spring of 1963, I spent almost a full year in negotiations with Frank and Dick Titelman. They were skillful bargainers, and they knew what their company was worth. Finally on March 11, 1964, we were able to announce that Puritan and Warner's had reached agreement on a merger. The price was about $10 million, the currency a cu-

The Late Sixties

Why do men who hate girdles like girls who wear Warner's?

At Warner's, we have a healthy regard for the female anatomy. We think a girl ought to look like a girl. Even in a girdle.

Too many girdles flatten where they should mold. They squash, squeeze and freeze a girl's flesh to stone. The look is unnatural, unfeminine. The girdles are anti-woman.

We think a girdle ought to help nature. Not fight it. Take that lacy paneled number on the right. It's not called Delilah for nothing. Three ounces of nylon and uncovered Lycra* spandex improve what needs improving—and leave the rest alone. You can always see the girl for the girdle. 10.95 is the price.

Incidentally, as you may have guessed, the people who run things at Warner's are Men.

Delilah by Warner's*

Another Warner's answer to sportswear; the all-stretch Delilah.

Fig Leaves and Fortunes

mulative preferred stock with each share convertible into one share of Warner's common.

Along with Puritan came its subsidiary unit, Thane, a marketer of higher priced, traditionally-styled men's sweaters and knit shirts. With Puritan and Thane we had achieved the position in men's sportswear we had been seeking.

But we still had only an insignificant share in the larger and faster growing field of women's sportswear. It would take many years, if ever, for us to build Lady Hathaway into national prominence. We needed something bigger, more immediate.

Among the best women's sportswear houses in the middle sixties was White Stag of Portland, Oregon. It was a leading brand in women's skirts, slacks, shorts, jackets, coats, sport shirts, warm-up suits, tennis and golf wear, as well as being the country's largest distributor of skiwear. It had a subsidiary, Hirsch-Weiss, which specialized in camping and water-sports equipment and was the American distributor of the popular Australian racing swimsuit, Speedo. Another subsidiary was Rosanna, one of the country's leading brands of women's fashion sweaters. Our research had shown just how good White Stag was, how important, how influential. It would be an ideal fit for us, and we coveted it with an enthusiam we had difficulty in concealing.

But there was a serious problem. Harold S. Hirsch, chairman, and Maurice Oppenheimer, his brother-in-law, through their own and their families' stock holdings, controlled 45.7 percent of the outstanding common, and a deal for White Stag was impossible without their approval. And that was tough. Several companies had attempted to buy White Stag, but Mr. Hirsch and Mr. Oppenheimer had proved to be reluctant bridegrooms. They could be brought to the altar, but they would not exchange vows. Our competitor, Genesco, which was rapidly expanding its apparel holdings, believed it had reached agreement to acquire White Stag, but the deal had come apart at the last minute. Maurice Oppenheimer, in particular, had proved obdurate. Observers of the industry, knowing our eagerness for White Stag, advised us not to try. "Wasting your time," they said.

Nevertheless, when the trust division of J.P. Morgan, which managed a block of non-family stock in White Stag and was nervous about the company's future, approached us in the summer of 1965 with their belief that a friendly take-over was possible, we decided to try. Several meetings between Harold Hirsch and Maurice Oppenheimer on their side and Fred Downey, our treasurer, and me produced some fragile hope for a possible agreement, but the obstacles were still formidable. Then we got a break. White Stag's key employees led a palace revolt. They had been disturbed by the "almost" sale to Genesco. They knew that Mr. Hirsch and Mr. Oppenheimer eventually would sell the company, and they worried to whom. Some of them told us, "They would sell to the Mafia if they got enough money." These employees, concerned about their own and the company's future, liked what they knew about Warner's and were aware of our good reputation in the marketplace and as employers. They felt that, if the company were to be sold, Warner's would be the preferred buyer, and they told Mr. Hirsch and Mr. Oppenheimer so. In turn, Mr. Hirsch and Mr. Oppenheimer knew that without their key people, the company would have to be sold at a discount. So they began to negotiate in earnest.

Harold Hirsch in particular not only had a substantial financial interest in White Stag, but a family one too. His father was one of the original founders in 1884 of its predecessor, the Willamette Tent and Awning Company. In those years it took at least 100 days for the clipper ships to sail from the East Coast to the West Coast. Arriving there, bat-

White Stag, which merged with Warner in 1966, featured casual sportswear, particularly slacks and jackets.

Fig Leaves and Fortunes

tered by the storms of the Atlantic, the Horn, and the Pacific, the ships sought refuge up
the Columbia River in the fresh-water port of Portland on the Willamette River. There
they could let their salt-water barnacles die in the "sweet water," after which the barnacles
could be easily scraped off the hulls, while the ships' crews sought their own refuge in the
bars and taverns of the city. Meanwhile the ships' sails had to be repaired or new ones made.
That was the job of the Willamette Tent and Awning Company, later the Hirsch-Weiss Canvas Products Company, named from its two founders, Mr. Hirsch and Mr. Weiss. This
canvas stitching company, in addition to sails, could make tarpaulins, tents, deck awnings,
and canvas bunks, anything made of canvas which a ship might need to return to sea.

Along about the turn of the century the logging industry descended on the virgin for-
ests of the Pacific northwest. Woodsmen from the cold climate of New England and the
north woods came to the warmer mountains and valleys of Oregon's Cascade and coastal
ranges. They were wearing their traditional heavy woolen mackinaws and work pants,
which promptly became damp, spongy, and hot in the mild, wet climate of the West.
Hirsch, Weiss had an answer to the problem. From the cotton canvas used for sails they
hacked water repellent coats and pants, and then dunked these sailcloth garments in boil-
ing paraffin or tallow until they became not only completely waterproof but so stiff that
they could stand up alone on the logging camps' bunkhouse floors. The garments were
promptly dubbed "tin pants" and "tin coats" and White Stag made thousands of them.

Young Harold Hirsch was sent east to college, to Dartmouth, in the late twenties and
early thirties. There he fell under the spell of the latest sports fad — skiing. But skiers, like
the earlier loggers, had a problem in finding proper clothing. Some simply used their hunting or fishing garb for skiing; some went to tailors who knew nothing about the new sport,
and a few, who could afford it, bought expensive imported Scandinavian, Swiss, or Austrian skiwear, designed by experts.

When Harold Hirsch returned to his family's business in Portland after college, he came
with an idea: he would combine his personal knowledge of the needs of an active skier
with Hirsch Weiss' practical experience in making work clothes to produce ski clothes that
were lightweight, sturdy, wind and water repellent, with freedom for action, yet good
looking.

He had other ideas too. The firm could not manufacture skiwear the year around, so
he proposed that it expand its design and production capabilities from skiwear into sportswear for other seasons. Accordingly it began making clothes for tennis, golf, swimming,
sailing, and hiking. To glamorize its new status as a sportswear company, its name was
changed from Hirsch Weiss to White Stag, simply a translation into English of the original German names of the founders. The original name was retained in the Hirsch Weiss
Canvas Products Company, a subsidiary making sleeping bags, air mattresses, tents, tarpaulins, etc., in reality a continuation of the original business founded long ago on the
banks of the Willamette.

Just as it was an emotional struggle for Warner's owners to become a public company,
so it was equally, or perhaps even more so, for Harold Hirsch to sell the family business,
which he had done so much to build. However, he had come to the conclusion that selling
was in his family's best financial interest, and when his key managers told him that they
favored Warner's as the buyer, he was able to convince his brother-in-law, Maurice Oppenheimer, through Herculean persuasion, to agree to a merger. An announcement was
made October 1, 1965, but final details were not confirmed until a special stockholders

The Late Sixties

meeting the following January. As in the case of Puritan, payment was made via a preferred stock convertible into Warner's common. Some 335,000 of the new shares were issued, which at $35 per Warner share (the current price on the New York Stock Exchange) made the transaction worth about $12 million.

In our 1965 annual report, I wrote, "The addition of White Stag provides the strong position in women's sportswear that we have been seeking and fulfills the primary goals of our diversification plan established some time ago. It also puts the Warner Brothers Company squarely among the five or six diversified apparel leaders that have emerged in recent years."

We had branched out into sportswear just in time. As the decade wore on, the fashion scene grew more turbulent; lightness, even semi-nudity, in clothing became universal. In spite of the new, lighter, and sheerer elastic fabrics which Warner's had developed, the girdle business took a dramatic plunge, replaced by pantyhose and bikinis. Fortunately for Warner's, the drop in sales of girdles was made up by increasing sales of shorts, slacks, and skirts of White Stag, sweaters of Rosanna, and men's slacks, shorts, and knit shirts of Puritan.

We had become a *Fortune* 500 company in 1965; in early 1968 we changed our corporate name from the Warner Brothers Company to Warnaco Inc. This was done to avoid confusion with other users of "Warners" in corporate titles and to distinguish the company name from "Warner's," the brand name of our well-known intimate apparel line, which we would continue to use.

In the nation the year 1968 was the "Year Everything Went Wrong" (the Tet campaign, withdrawal of Johnson, murders of Martin Luther King and Robert Kennedy, revolt of students at Columbia University), but for Warner's, now Warnaco, it was the year everything went right. Sales and profits reached an all-time high, $185 million and $7.7 million. In one year earnings per share had grown from $2.86 to $4.11. Since the beginning of diversification in 1960 the company's annual compound growth rate was 25 percent in sales and 24 percent in profits. In our annual report, I wrote, "This growth in size and profitability would appear to support the soundness of our expansion program."

One person who did not agree with that assessment was my father. He saw little that was good in what we had done. As chairman, he came to the office almost every day, a formidable presence just down the hall. As chairman, but with no management authority, eighty years of age, he retained an office and a secretary, attended almost all management meetings, invited or not. He talked to everybody, had opinions on everything, mostly contrary to mine. In my absence on business or vacation, he assumed the position of acting C.E.O. The board of directors knew of the conflict between us, but in deference to his years of service and contributions to the company did nothing to resolve it.

His opinions were usually expressed in memos to me. They were so often based on rumors and inaccurate information and phrased in such confrontational tones that they upset me.

For instance:

"To date your acquisitions have turned in no profit."

"I want to go on record as advising 100 percent that by continuing with . . . . . . (a top executive of the company) and giving him such authority as his five-year plan encompasses, you are not going to have a smooth working organization."

Fig Leaves and Fortunes

APRIL 1, 1965

VOGUE

"...the outline of the body
...the figure defined beneath a bias
of lace, organza, or chiffon"—in March
we called it the most prophetic thing in Paris.
On the brink of summer: the prophecy holds,
swells, *is.* The line of soft fabric flowing against a
clean, taut line of body is the line of today...the
strength of the body showing through transparent
clothes is the strength of fashion. For this moment...
for this era. The era's seductive herald, left: black
lace stretched over a look of naked strength,
swirled in chiffon—Heim *diablerie* on
a skin of Warner's Body Stocking.
Coiffure by Alexandre.

Vogue's Eye View: The Body Bulletin

A Vogue *editorial of April 1, 1965 on Warner's black stretch body stocking.*

The Late Sixties

"You have failed to organize along lines which use your existing people rather than new people brought in from the outside."

"The Corporation is being very extravagant, and there is great resentment."

"Operating divisions have very little respect for the personnel in your corporate group."

"You must realize that sooner or later your profits must justify your acquisitions and increase in corporate expense."

"I am flabbergasted that we should even consider adoption of such an extravagant program."

"I went over and had a talk with . . . . . (a salesman) this morning. As a result of this talk, I recommend very drastic action, and that action is that you put the Sportswear division into receivership."

" . . . . does not get along with any of the managers. He is very, very much disliked and feared by his own organization. If allowed to go much farther, he is going to wreck the corporation. Sometimes I think he is a mental case." (This was my father's opinion of a very able man who eventually left us and went on to a brilliant career in another company.)

"The return on the investment in this division does not justify our continuing to operate it."

"You should adopt a policy that is going to make the most money."

To most of these comments, I offered no answer. When I did reply, it was along the lines of, "I believe that today the stockholders of this company are being well served by their management. Running this company is a tough, hard, time-consuming job. We have dedicated people here, and I support them." Stung by an avalanche of criticism, on one occasion I responded tartly, "Your conclusions are based on inadequate and misleading information. However, I know you have strong feelings about them, and I think perhaps you should take action. As chairman of the board, in basic disagreement with the president, you should take the matter to the board with a recommendation of no confidence in the president. Otherwise, I think you should let me run this company the way I think it should be run. If what I am doing is wrong, if my policies are wrong, then it is up to the board to put in somebody else as president".

The chairman never brought the matter to the board.

In retrospect, this was the second time when I should have acted boldly to take over ownership of the company. The first was when we went public. Now, with our development program a success and with profits and sales at an all-time high, we were beginning to attract national attention. Several large corporations had offered to buy us, or merge with us. In 1968 there were 1,837,621 shares of Warnaco voting stock outstanding with the largest holders being inactive members of the Warner, Hirsch, and Titelman families. I myself owned only 9,396 shares; my father only 9,128. The rest of management owned little or nothing; we were all salaried workers, not owners.

On March 14, 1968, the closing price on the New York Stock Exchange for the company's stock was $31 1/8 per share. Earnings for the previous year were $3.67 per share. This meant that the stock was selling at 8½ times times earnings, or a value of $57 million for the whole company. Less than 20 years later it was to be sold for some $500 million.

The techniques of a leveraged buy-out had not been developed in 1968, but the people who approached to buy us or merge with us were prepared to borrow money to finance the deal. I am sure that we in management could have done the same thing, with security for the loan being the company's own assets. The Warner, Hirsch, and Titelman family members would have been willing, I am sure, to sell their stock for cash at a substantial profit, as would the public owners. In this way we in management could have taken control, freeing ourselves from a critical chairman, an irresolute board, and inactive family members, many of whom had lost interest in the company, except for the size of their dividends.

But we did nothing.

Instead, we basked in the glory of the attention we were getting. A California firm, Mitchum, Jones, and Templeton, wrote, "Under the direction of an imaginative management team, Warnaco has become a leading apparel manufacturer. Through acquisition, internal expansion, and product innovation the Company since 1960 has grown from a $31.4 million foundation garment manufacturer to a diversified apparel company with sales of $153.9 million in 1967."

Loeb, Rhodes & Co. of New York advised, "Warnaco should achieve record sales and earnings this year." Harris, Upham & Co. recommended "that the shares of this leading diversified apparel manufacturer be purchased in accounts seeking capital appreciation." Some of their reasons were:

"1) Projected entrance upon a period of rapidly expanding profit margins.

2) The projected impact of selected acquisitions, increasing revenues, and ensuring a dominant competitive position in a fragmented industry.

3) An excellent product mix, replete with established brand names.

4) An efficient operating structure, rare within the apparel field, coupled with an effective marketing organization. . . . Management has demonstrated its capacity to selectively acquire smaller companies which complement the existing structure, and its ability at the same time to maintain internal growth."

The Late Sixties

12

The Early Seventies

THE DECADE drew toward an end, but the passions of the sixties had not yet been spent; the years of new President Nixon's first term were marred by turmoil and disillusionment. The endless Vietnam War muddled on, and so did the anti-war demonstrations, the marches on Washington, the uproars on college campuses. Everywhere there was hostility to the "established order," whatever that was. The sexual revolution, the feminist movement, the racial problems, crime, drugs, domination by the young — they were all present. By 1970-71 the stock market was in decline, unemployment rising, international trade headed toward a deficit, the dollar tottering, recession at hand. In spite of it all, Nixon was reelected over a weak Democratic candidate, George McGovern, who was tarred as the advocate of "acid, amnesty, and abortion."

Until near the end of the sixties this national unrest found a mirror in fashion. Young women dressed in jeans or mini-skirts, devastating the market for girdles and exploding the market for pantyhose. Sportswear sales boomed; dress sales collapsed. Then, in sudden reversal as the seventies began, designers decreed the demise of the short skirt and dropped the hemline to mid-calf. Women of all ages, unaccustomed now to being minions to fashion, revolted at the sudden change, refused to wear the long skirts, and switched to pants and slack suits, thus clobbering the girdle market once again and for good measure bringing down the lingerie and pantyhose businesses with it.

In menswear the changes were almost as violent. Jeans were worn everywhere, as sales of suits fell and sales of slacks and sportshirts rose. Something called the "leisure suit," a shapeless coat and pant of polyester made its dramatic appearance, sold millions of units, then just as dramatically, and even more rapidly, disappeared. Fashion observers said, "Nothing that makes a man look so hideous can possibly last." They were right; millions of leisure suits had to be dumped overnight.

It was a frightening time to be in the apparel business. What to make? What styles?

When? In what quantities? What further changes were coming? This year? Next year? The turmoil was further stirred by major upheavals in retail distribution, as mass marketers and discounters took an ever larger share of the total market. Along with recession, inflation was coming. A shortage of U.S. labor, higher charges for what labor was available, and increasing prices for materials, all were resulting in higher costs.

To us at Warnaco all this suggested a need for a change in basic strategy. Up to 1968 we had concentrated on large firms with established brand names in areas of sustainable growth and stability, particularly in intimate apparel, men's shirts, and sportswear. This strategy had worked well for us, but we questioned whether, now in an era of rapid social, retail, and fashion revolution, it was still valid. We were shaken by the abruptness of fashion change and the way it suddenly accelerated or decelerated sales in a particular classification. We watched as changes in a nation's life style were reflected in current popular fashions, and, as we watched, we became convinced that safety lay in as complete a diversification of apparel products as possible. Men and women would wear "something"; "something" would be in style. Should we not make that "something?"

So it was that we drastically changed our marketing strategy. Instead of relying on a small number of major divisions, our new policy was to embrace more units in numerous classifications, trying to be ahead of fashion. We would plan to have the knowledge and facilities within our own organization to design and manufacture almost anything that men or women, in all their irrationality, might decide to wear. We would try to tame the fashion goddess.

It was a speculative and dangerous move, although at the time we did not realize just how speculative and dangerous it was. Actually we thought we were being conservative by not having all our eggs in one fashion basket.

We started out by filling what was the most obvious void in our product lines, pantyhose, which had devastated our Warner girdle sales. In an attempt to replace these lost sales, we entered the hosiery business by purchasing Concordia Leg Apparel, whose stockings and pantyhose were sold mostly in chain and discount stores and Beautiful Bryans, a subsidiary, with distribution in quality stores. In this way we not only joined the huge, highly competitive hosiery industry, but secured a foothold in the lower priced retail market, where our company as a whole had little representation.

Next we increased the variety of products marketed by our existing divisions. Puritan had been selling mostly knits made the full-fashioned way, but not all customers liked that kind of sportshirts and sweaters. So we bought Burkey Mills, a supplier of circular knits, and added its products to the Puritan line. The division sold no men's jackets, so we purchased Cresco Manufacturing Company, a maker of outerwear jackets in cloth and leather.

Hathaway was largely known for its woven dress shirts, so we acquired Quaker Knits, a knitting facility, and the push was on for Hathaway to sell knits as well as woven shirts. White Stag, although it sold a few sweaters and knitted shirts, was basically a producer of woven apparel. For them too we purchased a knitter, Medford Knitwear, which was also the owner of Playmore Knits, a producer and marketer of girls' sportswear. Up to that time White Stag had had no products for younger girls.

Not to be outdone, White Stag's subsidiary, Rosanna, a marketer of women's sweaters, went into the knit suit and dress business through an agreement with Corah, Ltd. of Great Britain, to market Corah's suits and dresses in the United States.

For this new strategy to succeed, we were aware that we needed instant and accurate

The Early Seventies

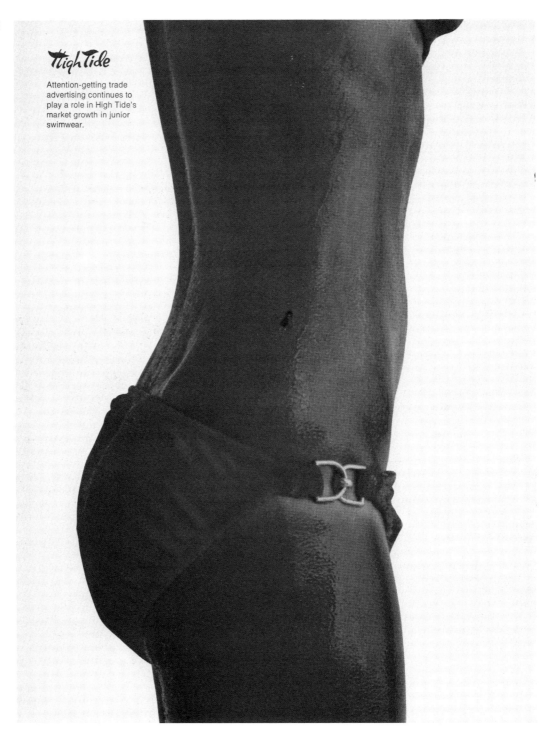

High Tide

Attention-getting trade
advertising continues to
play a role in High Tide's
market growth in junior
swimwear.

Diversification in the 1970s included High Tide's junior sportswear and swimwear.

Fig Leaves and Fortunes

fashion forecasting, and we came to believe that our insight into what was happening would be sharpened if we had more personal communication with retailers who had daily contact with customers. Accordingly we bought Gus Mayer Inc., a group of high-quality, high-priced, high-fashion, specialty stores located in Louisiana, Texas, Mississippi, Tennessee, Pennsylvania, Oklahoma, Kentucky, and California. Our rationale for this unusual move: "Retailing in the quality apparel field is a natural extension of our apparel manufacturing operations. We see market and design advantages in a closer relationship to retailing and a first-hand exposure to the always changing fashion markets."

Fashion forecasting was also a motivation in our acquisition of Jerry Silverman, Inc. of New York, a leader in the designer dress business on Seventh Avenue. I wrote, "Mr. Silverman's presence in the senior management of Warnaco will sharpen and quicken our fashion awareness and capabilities."

For simple diversification into a field where none of our divisions had an interest, we entered the exploding teen-age and junior sportswear business by buying Maro High Tide, a highly regarded producer of young swimwear and sportswear.

While we continued to diversify and add products in the early seventies, imports were becoming increasingly troublesome for almost all of our divisions. The lower costs of overseas producers, particularly in the Far East, landed merchandise in this country for far less than we could make similar styles here. In the years between 1966 and 1971 the percentage of imports of all women's sweaters increased from 23 percent to 57 percent. Imports of men's dress shirts were now 36 percent, up from 15 percent. Men's sportshirt imports were 30 percent, up from 8 percent. Our competitors and our customers were rushing to buy goods in Japan, Hong Kong, Taiwan, Korea, Singapore, and India. For their own protection our divisions began, one by one, to do likewise. Unfortunately these division merchandisers and buyers, visiting the Far East perhaps for the first time, were often neophytes in what could be a thieves' market. Too often they paid too much, received inferior merchandise, were late on delivery. Hurt by these mistakes caused by inexperience, we sought professional help in overseas buying, making arrangements with CBS Imports (no connection with *the* CBS), a large and experienced importer of apparel from the Far East, to purchase a minority interest in the firm and a three-year option to buy it outright.

CBS had offices and staff in Hong Kong, Japan, Korea, Taiwan and Singapore. They were, in effect, masters of the thieves, acting both as commission purchasing agents for large stores and buying for their own account for sales to mass merchandisers. The idea was that in the Far East our divisions would work through CBS, who would recommend source factories and help the division merchandisers get the best prices. Then CBS would keep careful watch on the selected plants to make sure quality was maintained and delivery schedules adhered to. CBS was profitable in its own right, so we would obtain this importing help at little cost while actually making money. In addition, as in the case of Concordia, they would provide us with further entry into the world of mass marketing and discount stores.

We were also prepared to "go international." We had always had a small international business, especially in Warner's, through world-wide licensing, but we now believed that there were opportunities for a Warnaco of Canada or a Warnaco of Europe to be established along the same lines as Warnaco, United States. Fashion was international, and so

The Early Seventies

we said, "In the years to come we will have need of a fashion communication network embracing most of the world."

For such a network, we started in Canada. There we had earlier acquired our licensees who had been making and distributing Warner's girdles and bras and Hathaway shirts. The former owner of Hathaway Canada, and still its president, James C. Walker, was put in charge of building and managing a Warnaco of Canada. Our first move was to buy the Croyden Manufacturing Company, Canada's largest manufacturer of men's and women's raincoats and an important producer of outerwear. This was followed by purchase of the Botnick Companies, licensees in Canada for White Stag skiwear, Speedo swimsuits, and High Tide swimwear. A little later Don Parker, maker of men's slacks, and then White Stag of Canada, licensee for White Stag's sportswear, were added, and to make the company more Canadian in feeling and ownership 30 percent of Warnaco of Canada was sold to the public, and the shares listed on the Toronto Stock Exchange.

A modest start was also made on what was hoped to be a Warnaco of Europe. A 34 percent interest in Jupiter of Paris was obtained, along with an option to buy control of this designer and distributor of rainwear and sportswear. A new production facility for Warner's was acquired in England through the purchase of Gordon Debrette, a girdle and bra maker in Nottingham, thus adding to the existing Warner's plants in Northern Ireland and Belgium. Finally, with an English partner, we formed a joint venture to market Hathaway shirts in Great Britain. On the other side of the world we purchased enough shares in Speedo of Australia to become the largest stockholder of that company.

This flood of new companies surged over us in the space of a very few years as Warnaco struggled to cover the apparel waterfront and to make itself invulnerable to fashion's whims. As can be imagined, the task of managing such a conglomerate became increasingly complex. The apparel industry is noted for the rampant egos of its managers, and our division heads were no exception. The problem was how to exert firm corporate control, especially in budgets and finances, while leaving freedom of action to our sometimes willful, but always entrepreneurial, division operators, who had to be held personally responsible for their individual divisions' results. To them, we could not dictate from headquarters. I wrote, "Each one of our 17 operating units has direct autonomy and responsibility for its own manufacturing, marketing, and merchandising. Bonuses for their managers are calculated on each unit's profitability, not the profitability of the company as a whole."

With the increased size and complexity of the company, I myself could no longer exert such corporate control. To help me, we moved Cameron Clark, hitherto the successful president of Warner Packaging, to senior vice-president for operations. Under him was a group of vice-presidents, all of whom were knowledgeable apparel executives. Lawrence Rennett, formerly president of White Stag, headed Womens' Wear. Gus Van Sant, recruited from the presidency of McGregor, a men's and boys' sportswear firm, supervised Mens' Wear. Harold Rudominer, who had come to us from our intimate apparel competitor, Playtex, to correct managerial and marketing weaknesses at Warner's, headed up Intimate Apparel. International was under James Gillies, formerly of Cannon Mills, who had been an able sales manager for Warner's. Each of these men had served for years in the "rag" trade, and I believed could provide the necessary supervision for our divisions without interfering in their day-to-day operations.

Fig Leaves and Fortunes

Nevertheless, as might have been expected, we had failures, most immediately, Concordia. It happened in 1970, a year which brought recession on top of the worst of fashion turbulence. In our annual report I commented, "Our businesses faced the most dramatic fashion and taste changes ever encountered." The catalyst for change was the drop of women's skirts from above the knee to mid-calf. As previously mentioned, women, in revolt, swore they would never wear a long skirt, abandoned dresses and skirts, and turned to pants and slack suits. The sales of pantyhose plummeted; there could be no doubt that we had entered the hosiery business at exactly the wrong time. With both fashion and the economic climate against us, we had to beat a hasty retreat. Hardly was the ink dry on our acquisition documents when we were faced with the need to eliminate Concordia. This we did at a cost of over $4 million including operating losses for 1970 and the estimated cost of liquidation. Concordia had proved an all too costly mistake.

Nor were the rest of our 1970 results satisfactory as the recession deepened. Retailers, faced with high inventories and slow sales, were reluctant to place orders, concentrating instead on reducing stocks. The result was a 50 percent drop in our profits from continuing operations and, with the Concordia charges, a final income of a mere $175,000, or four cents a share. We remained profitable for the year, but barely so.

Yet our optimism was not dimmed. I wrote, "It was a year in which our diversification policy proved its value . . . our present five-year plan aims at a volume of over $500 million by 1975 attained through internal development and selected acquisitions. We will continue to seek a balanced product mix and avoid the dangers of excessive concentration on specific styles and specific fashion looks."

As C.E.O. of Warnaco, I made mistakes. Without a doubt, I moved too far, too fast. I was rightly criticized for this, but ironically, in my own opinion, the *worst* mistake I made was something I *did not* do. Shortly after the merger with White Stag, I met with the president and principal owner of the H.D. Lee Company, manufacturer of Lee jeans. It was at the time when blue jeans were first exploding in the market, when it was apparent that with the casual life-style of the young and their anti-establishment mood, jeans were going to become the uniform of the American people. We had no producer of jeans among our Warnaco divisions; Lee was the third largest jeans brand in the country, behind only Levi and Blue Bell, and an obvious acquisition target for us or somebody else. I reached a tentative agreement to purchase Lee before checking back with our board of directors. There I faced disapproval. Two or three directors, including my father, did not think that buying Lee was a good idea, pointing out 1) that we had just merged with White Stag and had a lot to do to meld it in with Warnaco, and 2) that the Lee brand was strong mainly in retail basements and lower-priced stores, a different market from Warnaco's traditional one. There were also some questions about Lee's management. I am convinced that had I persevered, I could have won approval, but especially in view of the recent White Stag purchase, I yielded and passed up the golden opportunity. Shortly thereafter, our competitor, Vanity Fair, *did* buy Lee, and blue jeans rather than lingerie became the basis for their enormous success over the next many years. Since then I have often dreamed of what a fantastic company Warnaco would have been had we had a strong jeans brand to go with Warner's, White Stag, Puritan, Hathaway, and the rest.

The Early Seventies

Our bitter experience with Concordia warned us to be careful of areas we knew little about. Our management group had had no experience in hosiery; we had none in retailing, or, as a matter-of-fact, in packaging, even though we had been in packaging, as a company, but not as a management team, for many years. We simply did not have the expertise, nor the financial strength, to operate outside our own apparel ken. It was dangerous to try. Accordingly we made the decision to concentrate solely on apparel, to sell, in addition to our hosiery business, both our packaging division and our retail division. The first was done at a substantial capital gain; the second at a substantial loss. I wrote, "Selling Packaging is a particularly difficult decision because it has been a part of Warnaco for such a long time and because the people of Warner Packaging remain our close friends. But the decision was made, not only for Warnaco, but for them too. Packaging is out of our mainstream. It is becoming more difficult to give the division the financial support and the corporate attention it deserves. As part of Rexham Corporation, to whom we are selling Packaging, which is a company entirely in the packaging business, the division should get that attention."

Selling Gus Mayer was a different matter. In addition to the fact that we knew little about retailing, the present and potential return on investment had turned out to be inadequate to justify the injection of the further capital which would be needed to open new stores, modernize the ones we had, and stock all of them with the kind of merchandise now being demanded by customers. The Gus Mayer stores had been founded and grew in an era of elegance with designer and better dresses as the nucleus of their appeal. Now in an era of casual living and sportswear, they were still beautiful stores selling beautiful clothes, but they were old-fashioned too. Because their management did not agree with our ideas of modernization, we would have trouble transforming their stores to something more in tune with the times. It was better to let them go their own way and get rid of them.

While we abandoned efforts *outside* apparel, we were as determined as ever to have products in every growth area *within* apparel. And to have a top brand in each segment. As we surveyed our competitive position in the early seventies, we could see that, in addition to jeans, we had no position in the growing market for men's and women's contemporary sportswear. This was a sharp, unconventional look, far different from the traditional designs of a White Stag, a Jerry Silverman, or a Hathaway. The companies that were doing well in contemporary sportswear were mainly firms founded by young, with-it entrepreneurs. These new companies had reached astonishing sales volume and profits in quick time, and while some of them could be bought, their purchase prices were based not only on current, but on projected, profits. Those estimated future profits seemed imaginary to us. The risk of collapse for any one of them was just as great as the possibility of future success. We did not think it wise to buy into the business, but we did not want to be out of it either.

Our solution was to go out and find our own young entrepreneurs and finance them to start up new units in contemporary sportswear. If the new companies we were envying had been started from scratch, we reasoned we could do the same. The costs and risks would be far less than buying a speculative enterprise. We would control the new entrepreneurs by making them subsidiaries of one of our established divisions, through whom their budgets and expenses would be monitored.

Accordingly, we created four new, small companies selling contemporary sportswear. Hathaway and White Stag were eager to pioneer, so Hathaway started Hathaway Other-

Fig Leaves and Fortunes

wear to make off-beat clothes for men and Hathaway Patch to do the same for women, and White Stag launched Allison's Closet for very young contemporaries and Liz Carlson for their older sisters. Out of these beginnings the odds seemed to favor our getting at least a couple of successes.

As the 1970 recession disappeared and some of the fashion chaos abated, things turned up for Warnaco. By 1973 we were completing our 100th year in business and the best single year in sales and profits. In our annual report we could boast, with some justification, that "Warnaco's group of brands is probably the most unique and outstanding combination of apparel products in any corporate organization. *Warner's* is to this day one of the great international brands in slimwear. *White Stag* is one of the best known names in women's sportswear and the world's largest manufacturer of skiwear. *Puritan* is the dominant brand in men's knit sport shirts and sweaters. *Hathaway*, in business continuously since 1837, is the by-word for quality men's dress shirts. *Rosanna* is one of the leading brands in women's sweaters, knitwear, and contemporary styles. *High Tide* is a similarly dominant name in junior swimwear. *Jerry Silverman* is a special name in fashion dresses. *Playmore* is a leading brand in girlswear. *Hirsch-Weiss* uses sewing skills to manufacture a top line of tents, sleeping bags, and backpacks as well as watersports equipment like wet-suits, and also markets *Speedo* racing swimsuits of Olympic fame. *Cresco* is a maker of quality men's leather and cloth outerwear. *Thane* is a label of special prestige on men's sweaters and knits. *Croyden* is Canada's largest rainwear maker and a leading outerwear producer. *Don Parker* is Canada's leading men's slacks and coordinates house."

It was indeed a pinnacle. Since the start in 1960 of the expansion and diversification program sales had grown tenfold. Earnings per share had increased at a compound rate of 7.3 percent annually, in spite of our major investments in new products and new markets, and better than the average for all American industry. We had products in almost all apparel classifications, especially the current life-style favorite, sportswear. Our distribution was in department stores, specialty stores, chains, and mass merchandisers. We had a growing international business. Our three-year plan called for a volume of over $500 million and a doubling of 1973 profits.

In its issue of October 15, 1974, *Forbes* magazine, often a stern critic of business, called Warnaco "that rare thing, a well-managed garment company." It offered its opinion that "if Warnaco isn't wholly impervious to the slings and arrows of outrageous fashion, it is seldom hurt badly by them either."

Unfortunately *Forbes* was wrong. We were about to be hurt badly.

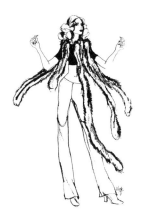

The Middle Seventies

*T*HE WAR in Vietnam finally ended, and the communists took over that unfortunate country. The worst recession since the thirties, combined with mounting inflation, shook business and the every-day lives of every-day people. Nixon imposed a price freeze to try to control inflation, but he could do little about unemployment, which rose to 9.2 percent, a thirty-three year high. The Arabs, unhappy with the U.S. role in the Yom Kippur war, declared an oil embargo, and the resulting energy crisis produced long lines and ill tempers at the nation's gas stations.

All this, plus Watergate, devastated Nixon and the Republican party. He resigned as president in August 1974, and in spite of the best efforts of his quiet successor, Gerald Ford, to calm things down, the Democrats swept the Congressional elections of that year and then in 1976 captured the presidency with Jimmy Carter. The mood of the country was "get rid of the rascals"; whoever was in, was out.

In accord with this national disorder, fashion continued on its own erratic course. The mini-skirt was gone but jeans and beads were still in. In such turbulent times there was a reluctance to return to the traditional; eccentric fashion prevailed over basics. It was a period of sudden innovation, sudden success, and sudden failure. Men's white shirts sold poorly, but colored and boldly patterned open-necked shirts moved rapidly out of the stores. Basic sweaters were dull; as *Forbes* magazine put it, "The guys wanted fashion sweaters depicting Mount Everest, the Empire State Building, or Jaws." Dress sales were still weak, and Paris had not regained its influence. *Vogue* wrote, "The petticoat went out of fashion, bras were not obligatory, sales of panties dropped, nightwear was no longer of primary importance . . . this winter's bras no longer hide anything; with their matching briefs they resemble bikinis. Girdles are unfashionable."

It remained a dangerous time to be in the apparel business. Not only was business poor, costs rising, but what people were going to buy and wear was wildly speculative. Howev-

Warner's and Hathaway acquired the license to make Dior shirts in 1974 and other Dior products have been added since.

The Middle Seventies

er, with Warnaco's multitude of products in a multitude of markets we felt secure, confident, as we had said before, that "men and women would wear something," and that we were well positioned, and had the skills, to take advantage of what that "something" was.

The first part of 1974 did nothing to shake our confidence. Sales reached an all-time high. Operating profit for the first three quarters was slightly ahead of the previous record year. In addition, we had added two promising new brands—Days of Tacoma, Washington, a manufacturer of men's slacks and of the then popular leisure suits and Stern, Merritt Co. of New York, a tie manufacturer whose connections with Christian Dior-Paris enabled us to obtain the license to make and sell Dior men's shirts, ties, and handkerchiefs in the United States. With these products, plus the future addition of other Dior products, we were destined to become the largest Dior licensee in the world. And a highly profitable relationship it would prove to be.

But the last quarter of 1974 was a disaster. As the nation headed into the eye of the recession, the stores began a massive drive to reduce inventories through price promotions, even as the all-important Christmas season was approaching. The result was a sharp decline in reorders and in basic, full-price merchandise. What merchandise we did ship was mostly off-price. Our fourth quarter operating profit dropped 55 percent.

To add to our woes, we ran into snags in attempting to sell the Gus Mayer stores. We had already recorded an anticipated loss of $1,300,000 in our 1973 figures, but the two purchasers to whom we had contracted to sell the stores experienced financial and legal difficulties, and it proved impossible to collect from them more than their already-deposited cash down payments. So we had to take another $3,400,000 of write-downs which, together with the fourth quarter weakness, reduced our yearly net revenue to $5,689,000, off almost 50 percent from the year before.

In spite of our year-end disappointment, we could take consolation from the fact that our operating income in 1974 was the second-best ever, but there was no doubt that, perhaps for the first time, our confidence was being shaken. We had had outstanding performances from many of our divisions, but too many others were failing to meet their goals. Things were simply not falling into place the way they should. We needed a comprehensive strategic review to see where we had come from, where we were, and where we were going.

This review, started in the summer of 1974, highlighted a number of weaknesses that had been ignored in our rush to add brands, products, and sales volume, all in our quest to defang fashion. It showed that we were not producing enough cash to finance further expansion or even to support normal sales growth. We could not raise additional capital through sale of stock inasmuch as the price of our common on July 1, 1974, after the best profit year in our history, was only $10 per share with a price-earnings ratio of a puny 4-1. This meant that the financial community valued Warnaco at only $40 million at a time when we were carrying inventory worth over $90 million and had a book value of $84 million. Raising money through additional borrowings was also impossible. We were carrying as much debt as was prudent.

We would simply have to get whatever funds we needed out of a positive cash flow from current operations, but getting money that way was not easy. I wrote in July 1974, "All these projections for improved cash flow and profits assume that we make our 1974 budgets. Yet I have grave doubts about our ability to do so. While the divisions have been reasonably successful in meeting their sales projections, their ability to meet cash flow and profit objectives has been weak. They have been utilizing more assets than they needed or planned, mostly inventories and accounts receivable. This must stop."

But it did not stop. Excess inventories, almost inevitably resulting in markdowns, were our biggest bugaboo. Our divisions were manned mostly by merchandisers and marketers, which was probably correct for a fashion apparel company where being fashion-right was a priority, but too often their concentration on volume adversely influenced their business judgment. Too often our divisions regarded sales growth as a goal in itself, regardless of the amount of assets employed. Such an objective, I pointed out, was not compatible with corporate needs, but it seemed as if I whistled in the dark.

I can give an example. I have mentioned the leisure suit before. This unfortunate fashion emerged in 1973, sold in big volume during 1974 and most of 1975, and then abruptly collapsed, leaving inventory chaos in its wake. Our new acquisition, Days, was involved with it in a big way. As the demand for leisure suits mounted higher and higher, stores placed more and more orders with anybody who showed them even passable samples, duplicating orders unmercifully. Thus Days had far more orders than they could fill and were scrambling to make or buy more of both tops and bottoms.

It was a bubble bound to burst, but Days did not see it that way. To them it simply meant increased immediate volume. My file is full of pleas to Cameron Clark and Gus Van Sant, group vice-president for menswear, begging them not to let Days' merchandisers get stuck with inventory when the leisure suit fashion crashed. For instance, on September 25, 1975, I wrote, "I admit to continued nervousness on the leisure suit business. Believe me, there is going to be a reaction to this deplorable fashion. I am so afraid of Days getting stuck with thousands of dozens of leisure suits. They are very late in delivery, and I am convinced the stores will get overstocked and cancel what has not been delivered. Please, let's not get stuck. I think it is up to both of you and Mindy [Mindy Slikas, president of Days] to see that it doesn't happen."

Unfortunately it *did* happen. My warnings, and maybe the warnings of Clark and Van Sant, apparently never got down to the merchandisers and stockkeepers at Days, or possibly they just thought I was wrong and that the leisure suit fashion would last forever. Our loss in too many leisure suits ran into the millions of dollars.

As in the case of problems with my father, it is extremely difficult — and painful — for me to write about the events of 1975-76. Certainly we had gone too far, too fast in building an apparel conglomerate. Certainly we did not find the safety from fashion change which we had sought in a variety of products. Certainly the resulting lack of sales and excess inventories hurt us badly. Certainly our management, especially I myself, could be faulted for poor judgment.

But we had our share of bad luck too. Our weaknesses came to a head at a time of severe recession and at a time when we were encountering a number of non-operating problems. These included the need to sharply increase estimated taxes because of an imbalance between domestic profits and profits in Puerto Rico, where many of our divisions had plants. Also there was a claim by U.S. Customs against White Stag for several million dollars of penalty for so-called violations of importing regulations. In addition, Warnaco and our subsidiary, CBS, appeared on the front page of the *New York Times* as the recipients of termed illegal rebates from an ocean freight carrier. All of these matters were eventually resolved in our favor, but coming, as they did at a time of declining operating results, compounded our distress.

It was perhaps ironic that many of our 1975 problems were caused by the very thing we had created our organization to avoid: violent changes in fashion. It was the peak year for fashion's swing away from basic merchandise to high style, new, and innovative items. Some of our divisions reacted faster than others to these changes, conforming their products and inventory management to the fluctuating markets. Others were slow to recognize what was happening. Our biggest problem was Puritan, normally a producer of basic men's shirts and sweaters, which found it difficult to design, make, and sell fashion goods, and which ended the year in an inventory bath. Hathaway too had its problems, not moving aggressively enough from basic dress shirts to the fashionable sport shirt market. To bolster Hathaway's management we persuaded Robert Matura, an executive at Jockey in Milwaukee, whom we had known for some years and for whom we had considerable admiration, to leave Jockey and join Hathaway as president. Matura was to play an important role in Warnaco's future.

The losses in these two divisions, plus losses at the Medford Mill where basic goods sold to chain stores had suffered, amounted to close to $7 million, by themselves ensuring a poor profit year. Nevertheless, in December I proposed to the directors that we pay the regular twenty cent per share dividend, reasoning that the worst of the recession and the fashion changes seemed to be over. Christmas business in the stores was good, with our fourth quarter shipments up and profits improved. The budgets for 1976 were encouraging; if we were not optimistic, we were at least mildly heartened.

So we entered the fatal year, 1976, with most of our divisions doing well. At the end of the first six months I could report that "Warners, Rosanna, SW-1, and Hirsch-Weiss are continuing their steady upward trend. White Stag's women's sportswear is performing well, as is Hathaway and its tie division, Stern Merritt. High Tide swimwear is profitable. CBS is contributing handsomely to earnings. International, including Canada, may have a record year."

But problems in the other divisions were mounting. Days was incurring sharp losses as it liquidated its leisure suits, not having paid attention to warnings. Puritan, burdened with excessive productive capacity for basic goods, was selling off substantial stocks of misguided fashion sportswear, fashion sweaters, and its own leisure suits. Several of our new, small units, successful from a design and prestige point of view, were losing start-up money. Medford was in the red. The cash flow problem had not been solved.

In the spring of 1976 I wrote a memo to myself as the basis for a discussion with the board. Its title was "Why has our profit record been so unsatisfactory and erratic over the last five years?" I pinpointed three reasons.

1) Too many products and product lines.
2) Failure to respond quickly to fashion changes.
3) Poor inventory and production controls.

There may have been other reasons, but these were the most important. We had tried to cure these weaknesses by looking to individuals to straighten things out, by removing one manager and putting in another. There was no doubt that the right division manager made all the difference, but it was dangerous to expect that we could always have the right individual in the right job, especially because we were expecting each division president

Fig Leaves and Fortunes

to be both a fashion merchandiser and a good businessman. Such paragons were few and far between.

Another thing. As in the leisure suit case, we at corporate headquarters were constantly offering suggestions or warnings to the divisions which were not heeded. I believed I myself had been reasonably skillful in anticipating economic upturns and downturns, lifestyle and fashion changes, and in accordance, had suggested sensible policies to the divisions for inventory, cash flow, products, and marketing procedures. But these suggestions rarely got implemented and only with painful slowness. Why?

Probably because of our organizational structure: the long chain of command from me through Cameron Clark, our president, through one of our group vice-presidents, through the division president, down to the merchandising, production, selling, or financial departments of the division involved. Along this long line our suggestions or warnings were too often lost, altered, or ignored.

Then I took a frank look at myself. For me it was a time of true anguish. I had made the company my life's work, had a large share in building it, believed in it, *still* believed in it, perhaps even more than ever. What everybody involved was forgetting, in the depression of the moment, was the importance of what *had* been built. From an obscure corset company we had created a great American enterprise, a Fortune 500 company, the envy of the retail and apparel trades. We were experiencing difficulties, but they could be corrected. It was still true, as we said in our 1973 report, that "Warnaco's group of brands is probably the most unique and outstanding combination of apparel products in any corporate organization." My task was to preserve that organization while returning it to profitability.

But was I the man to do this, to make the necessary changes? Was I a better entrepreneur than day-to-day manager? Were the mistakes I had made so serious that they were impairing my effectiveness as a leader? Had I been C.E.O. long enough — eighteen years? Yet, even if all this was true, I *did* know the company better than anybody else. I *did* know fashion and the whims and ways of the apparel business. I still had a lot to contribute. But did I need help?

So I reasoned with myself and came to a conclusion, hard for me to accept but necessary for the company. Yes, I *did* need help. A new management team should be appointed which would combine the entrepreneurial flair and knowledge of the fashion and apparel markets which I still possessed with the operating skills of an experienced executive. It was time for me to bring in a manager who could lead such a team and then succeed me as C.E.O. Unlike my father, I would not wait for the board to push me out.

The logical new leader was Cameron Clark, now president. He had been an able, hardworking, devoted Warnaco executive for many years and wanted to be C.E.O. But the results under his leadership as head of operations had not been very good. Whether he had the skills, or the requisite in-depth knowledge of the fashion and apparel business, to execute the required changes seemed questionable. In any case, his position was weakened, as mine was, by the unsatisfactory current conditions.

These were some of the thoughts I brought to a small group of the board during the spring of 1976 as operating results failed to improve. I was not surprised to find that most of them believed it was time for a change in Warnaco management, and that they were not enthusiastic about Clark as C.E.O. As an alternative, I suggested that we bring in a new team consisting of James Walker, who had so successfully helped us to build and manage Warnaco of Canada, and Philip Lamoureux, president of Warner's, who had an enviable record in managing our still most profitable division. Jim had started a small shirt company in Prescott, Ontario, which had become the Hathaway Canadian licensee. Subsequently he had sold his company to Hathaway before we acquired that company, had been marketing director of Hathaway U.S.A., then returned to Canada when Hathaway, in dire financial stress, gave his company back to him. Finally I myself had again bought Hathaway from him, this time for Warnaco, and appointed him president of Warnaco Canada, as that embryonic enterprise got underway. Presently he was a director of Warnaco, U.S.A., so our other directors knew him well. With his skill in handling major conceptual issues and outside interests, I believed he would make an ideal president and eventual C.E.O.

While Jim would be "Mr. Outside" in the new organization, Phil Lamoureux would be "Mr. Inside." Phil had spent all his working life with Warner's, having joined the company straight out of college. He had been a production manager, inventory control manager, president of Intimate Apparel, the Warner's subsidiary doing business with chain stores, and subsequently president of Warner's. His strength was in handling detail.

Neither Jim nor Phil knew Warnaco well. With my knowledge of the company, the markets, and the industry, my task would be to help them get to know and understand the whole of Warnaco and its people, plus assisting on long-range planning. Together, I believed that the three of us, working as a team, could do what had to be done to restore stability and profitability to Warnaco. I would remain C.E.O for a few months while the new team got oriented, at which time Walker would become president and C.E.O with Lamoureux as executive vice-president and chief operations officer. I would be chairman until my regular retirement date in 1979 at the age of sixty-five, when Walker, if all went well, would become chairman and Lamoureux president. Clark would immediately become vice-chairman, though the expectation was that he would prefer to find some other job.

After considerable discussion, the members of the board approved of my recommendations, and on June 25, 1976, they voted for the proposed management changes.

14

Into the Eighties

 O IT WAS Jimmy Carter and "human
aspirations" and unconditional pardon for
Vietnam draft evaders and Camp David
and soaring inflation and interest rates
at all time highs and gold at over $800 an ounce and silver at $35 and hostages in Iran and
finally in 1980, Ronald Reagan, the former movie actor. But business was a lot better than
it had been a few years earlier.

In fashion there was a sort of return to normalcy, extremes being suddenly out, and
Paris beginning to regain some of its influence. Dresses and tailored suits, more closely
cut, became fashionable again, and along with the return of grand evening dresses brought
a mild revival in the girdle business. The rounded bra once more sold well, usually with
wiring to hold its cutaway cups in place. Men's suits and business shirts picked up volume.

At Warnaco things did not go as I had hoped. It was my understanding that as a builder of the company and still chairman of the board, I would be part of the new management team. I had brought Jim Walker down from Canada to work with me and Phil
Lamoureux to correct our problems and restore Warnaco to profitability. But they turned
out to have ideas quite different from mine. I regarded the difficulties of 1976 as a serious
downturn in the long-time progress of the company, but not sufficient reason to change
its entire concept. Yes, we had to sharply cut expenses, concentrate on controlling inventories and cash flow, pay down our debt, even liquidate some of our weaker units, but
not initiate a wholesale destruction of what had gone before. They saw a completely
changed Warnaco with the elimination of many of our businesses, a Warnaco comprised
of only a very few major divisions, with a skeleton corporate staff. In my building of the
company, I had been thinking of the long future, believing in an apparel company with
a variety of products serving many fashion markets and distribution systems. They proposed to operate a company with only a few large, immediately profitable, units. What
counted for them were profits today, not tomorrow. With such different points of view,
it was unlikely that Jim, Phil, and I could work smoothly together.

It is a business axiom, when managements change, for the new management to blame all the problems on the old management. The usual technique for doing this is to take as many losses and reserves as the accountants will permit, charging these deductions against the current year and the old management, thus creating recoveries in subsequent years in order to provide profits for the new management. This is what Jim and Phil did in 1976.

Actually the year would not have been a good one anyway for Warnaco, but certainly not the complete disaster it was eventually portrayed. The continuing divisions had a combined operating profit of more than $3 million. Sales reached an all-time high of $393 million, while nine of our fourteen divisions had profits higher than the previous year and three of them set records for sales and earnings. Nevertheless Jim and Phil took dramatic action to change things.

In quick order, they sold or liquidated Liz Carlson, Hathaway Patch, Hathaway Otherwear, Cresco, and the Medford Mill, some of which had future potential, but most of which were currently losing money. They closed Puritan and Days operations in Mexico, Texas, and North Carolina. At corporate headquarters they cut payrolls by a million dollars, almost immediately dismissing group vice-presidents, Gus Van Sant and Bill Seldon, encouraging the resignation of Fred Downey, financial vice-president, and giving former president, Cameron Clark, a meaningless staff job. They also eliminated the corporate departments of production engineering, research and planning, public relations, and management development. The trade paper, *Daily News Record*, reported enthusiastically, "with the cold perspective of surgeons they pruned firms, plants, and personnel."

The cost of all these firings, plus the booking of estimated additional taxes and the $14.2 million charge to cover the proposed liquidation of divisions, resulted in a reported loss for Warnaco in 1976 of $23,326,000. Walker wrote, "Warnaco had a very bad year in 1976. Action has been taken to see that it is one of a kind . . . that there will be nothing like it again."

I did not agree that such a huge loss for 1976 reflected the true condition of the company. The liquidation of so many divisions and the elimination of so much valuable corporate staff seemed to me extreme and an over-reaction to the situation, but my position was a difficult one. I was up against a general feeling among the directors and the banks that while the old management had built a good company, the new management could operate it better and should have an opportunity to do what it wanted to do. With such an opinion generally held, Walker's and Lamoureux's wishes on dispositions and staff reductions prevailed.

On January 1, 1977, Jim was made president and C.E.O. while I remained chairman. Logically, we should have worked together, but he did not want such a partnership, preferring to ignore me as chairman and to discuss his ideas with a newly created advisory committee of the board, which he had appointed from among his board friends and which was gradually taking over the role of the chairman. He wanted it clearly understood within the company and outside that *he* was now in charge.

He made this dramatically clear to me on the afternoon of Wednesday April 6, 1977. I was working late at my office in Bridgeport, having returned from a trip among the divisions, when a call came through from Walker at his vacation home in Florida. He told me brusquely that he was disturbed by my visit to the divisions and with my attitude: obviously I was unhappy with my role at the company and with my relationship with him. My continued contact with the divisions was interfering with him and Phil.

Fig Leaves and Fortunes

"I am sorry, Jim. I am unhappy," I answered. "I am still chairman of this company and therefore have considerable responsibility for what goes on here."

"You forget that you are no longer in charge," he interrupted. "When you visit a division, they do not know what you are doing there and who is running things."

"When I visit a division I do not tell anybody what to do. I tell them you are in charge, and any orders must come from you or Phil. But I have known most of these people for a very long time. They are my friends. Most of them I put in their jobs. I know the way they think and what they think. And sometimes I can suggest ideas to them that might be useful."

"Well, I do not think that anything you can say now would help. I have made up my mind that I am forbidding you to talk to the divisions — to the division president, or to the people in the division. Or to have any access to division files, reports, or correspondence. You are to stay completely away from the divisions. Any information you want, about anything, must come from me or Phil."

I could not believe what Jim was saying. I protested, "This order is cruel and unfair. The people *want* to talk to me. They know that I know what they are talking about. It's true I have been unhappy about what is going on, and this order of yours makes me more unhappy. I want to help because this company is my life but you won't let me."

Jim was adamant. "Jack, that's the way it is. Phil and I are running this company, and you are not. If you do not like it, you can take it up with the board, with your friends on the board, and talk with them about your role in the company."

Toward the latter part of this conversation tempers grew heated, and we agreed it was time to end it and discuss the matter at another time. I did talk to most members of the board, but their attitude was that Walker was now C.E.O. and they would have to either support him or remove him. I also talked to Phil with whom I had worked for many years and for whom I had considerable respect. His advice was succinct. "Find something else to do and let us make money for the company!"

In a sense, it was an ironic moment. While my father was still active, I had tried for years to gain control of the company. Perhaps I too had been a little cruel when I had thought it necessary to establish my own authority. Perhaps now I could understand better than before how he felt about being pushed aside. But I had never treated my father the way Jim was treating me. In fact, even now, in 1977, at age ninety, John Field was still honorary chairman and had his office and secretary down the hall (he died in 1979 at the age of ninety-two, still with a Warnaco office). I had tried so hard to treat him kindly for all his past contributions; never would I have dreamed of ordering him to keep away from his friends in the business. As a contrast, in one short minute, without regard for emotion or sentiment or long service, Jim Walker had cast me aside.

The situation did not change in the next year or two. Jim and Phil held a meeting for division presidents in Florida in December 1977. I was not invited. It was the first such meeting in over thirty years I had not attended. My file is full of remonstrances to Jim, of reminders that I did not like what was going on. I wrote, "I am terribly worried about this company. It is a different kind of company than it was two or three years ago. It is crassly materialistic. Respect, loyalty, and affection for individuals have disappeared. Long-time contributions are forgotten. Employees are terminated suddenly and often without cause. Some hang on because they have years of service and for them to be fired or quit would be financially disasterous. Instead they hunker down and either agree with what-

Into the Eighties

ever edict comes down from above or simply hope they won't be noticed. There is no spirit of teamwork; sentiment is gone.

"The style of management has changed. Instead of an open top management team, receiving input from many sources, we have two men making all the decisions. The company is being operated on a very short time span. Everything is done for today's profits; tomorrow is largely forgotten. Little advance planning is taking place. Nobody answers the question of what kind of company we are or what kind of company we will be tomorrow. The board, blinded by recent favorable financial results, sees nothing, is told nothing, and does nothing."

My personal feelings are reflected in a handwritten note I gave to Jim Walker in June of 1979, the year I was due to retire as chairmen and an employee, and, unlike my father, move out of the Warnaco building. "I don't believe you will ever begin to understand how I have felt the last two or three years. As I have said so often, this company has been my life. I realize I am a sensitive person. But rightly or wrongly, I have been deeply hurt by the way I have been treated. To be ignored is the worst form of humiliation. I believe my knowledge of this company and of the industry could have been put to good use. But my advice has not been asked.

"I hate to end my 30 odd years at Warnaco with the bitterness and disappointment I feel. I thought when you came down from Canada that we could work together. But obviously you did not want that to be. I am sorry."

Jim never did respond to this note.

The question will be asked why I did not resign. Certainly that was what Walker wanted, but in a strange way I did not want to give him that satisfaction. More importantly, I had my own future, and that of my family, to worry about. I was not a wealthy man. My salary and bonuses at Warnaco had always been modest, as my father's had been. Neither he nor I had ever owned a substantial number of Warnaco shares of stock, and unfortunately I had sold some of my shares to educate our children, and perhaps support a lifestyle richer than prudent, assuming in a somewhat reckless way, as my father had done, that somehow the company would take care of me. I have mentioned before that I failed to take advantage of opportunities which might have existed to make a substantial sum of money by taking the company private and securing a control position. I had few outside investments; my projected pension was only $42,000 a year. Some of my stock options had been cancelled and my incentive pay eliminated because, Jim said, I had "retired early." As a result of all this, I would be financially dependent in the future on a consulting contract signed in 1983 between me and the company. This contract, later extended by Bob Matura when he was C.E.O., was a generous one and ran until I was eighty years old, but could be cancelled by the company if I resigned before my official retirement date. I had no doubt that this is what would have happened had I quit.

In addition, there was another reason I refused to resign. I *still* believed I could contribute something to the company which I had helped build, and that perhaps the time to do so would *still* come. Meanwhile I had to swallow my pride, keep my balance and sense of humor, and ride out the storm.

Walker and Lamoureux made a harmonious team. Walker was the front man, the public relations man, the contact with the banks and the financial community. Beyond that he did little with operations. That job fell to Phil, the internal managing director, the detail man, who on a day-to-day basis operated the company. Divorced and a current bachelor, he set out on an endless travel circuit of the divisions, meeting continually and personally with each division president to discuss plans, budgets, products, mark-ups, grosses, expenses, and profits. Phil was the helmsman, the only person at corporate headquarters with whom the divisions had to be concerned. Unquestioned loyalty to him was demanded.

In accord with their concentration on profits, on which their bonuses were calculated, both Jim and Phil were impatient with the divisions. They wanted favorable results today, not tomorrow. If a division could not produce satisfactory profits now or in the short future, it was sold or liquidated. There was little or no attempt to fix a business. Fixing took time and involved risks, which the new management was not inclined to take. In addition to the divisions closed in 1976 other divisions soon felt the ax. Jerry Silverman, a fixture in a conservative woman's fashion wardrobe, was sold after an abortive attempt to have it design and make sportswear, which was simply not in its image. High Tide, a junior swimsuit company, not currently returning a satisfactory profit, but a business with high potential and popular with the stores and its young customers, was liquidated. Linwood Melton, president of High Tide, departed Warnaco and immediately started his own junior swimsuit and sportswear firm and did very well. Hirsch-Weiss was taken out of the camping and water-sports business, where it had a dominant position, so the company could concentrate on Speedo. CBS Imports, temporarily hurt by rising interest rates but still profitable, was also liquidated. Its president, Jack Clark, like Melton, soon went back into his same old business and made another fortune. All in all, over $200 million in volume was removed from the Warnaco sales base.

I sat helplessly by, watching the company we had created dissolved piece by piece.

With an absence of investment in the future, and concentration on the most profitable divisions, current results were spectacular. In 1977, the first year following the 1976 debacle, Warnaco had a net profit of $7,059,000, produced materially by reversal of unneeded reserves taken to raise 1976 losses. The years 1978 and 1979 were even better, as in the latter year record highs were recorded in profits. Again a substantial contribution was made by the reversal of reserves. Results were so good that even Jim and Phil were willing to admit that for them to produce such profits so quickly, the company must have been built on solid foundations.

By the end of the decade, Warnaco was a changed company. In my opinion, and in the opinion of a few other knowledgeable observers, it was not as good a company, being harvested to produce immediate profits. I pleaded with Jim and Phil to consider the future, when profits in major divisions like Warner's and Hathaway could no longer be ballooned by increasing margins, reducing advertising and promotions, and eliminating personnel. Such pleas always failed.

For the present, at least, they were producing results. As the decade of the seventies ended, and the 1980s began, the company was booming. In spite of a world-wide recession in 1981 and 1982, accompanied by unprecedented inflation with sky-high interest rates, new Warnaco records were set yearly.

With such results, national and international laurels were bestowed on Warnaco's management, especially on Jim Walker. In 1982 he was named "Apparel C.E.O of the Year" by *Financial World Magazine* and "Best Chief Executive — Apparel Industry" by the *Wall Street Transcript*. He was elected a director of Warnaco's lead bank, the First National Bank of Boston, and of Phillips Cable Ltd. in Canada, as well as first vice-chairman of the Ameri-

Into the Eighties

can Apparel Manufacturers' Association. In recommending the purchase of Warnaco stock, Kidder Peabody wrote glowingly about Walker and said the "company management has a very definite business approach: it is focused, disciplined, creative, and strongly geared to the bottom line." Walker himself gave interviews to several newspapers and magazines resulting in accolades to himself and brick-bats to our old management. *Forbes* commented that "Under former Chairman John Field the old-line corsetier had wound up in more awkward situations than the ever-dreaming, competing Maidenform woman." And later, "He used Warnaco's cash flow to push the unfamiliar brand names of a series of small, diversified acquisitions, and fell flat on his face." I believed both of these opinions came from Walker himself, but he denied it. In any case, had I desired to resign, such public criticisms would have made it nearly impossible for me to find another job in the apparel industry.

Buoyed by the company's success, the board of directors rewarded Walker generously. In 1982 he earned $820,297 in salary, fees, and bonuses, and had over $2 million in realized and unrealized gains from stock options.

But there was a darker side to Warnaco during these years. So many changes, often unexpected and sudden, at corporate and in the divisions, had a corrosive effect on employee morale, especially on those who had been with the company for many years, some for an entire working lifetime. As operating units were spun off, sold, or liquidated, and as corporate departments vanished, many employees found themselves without jobs, their careers in shambles. To many observers, and certainly to those employees personally involved, management's attitude seemed cold and indifferent.

Sometimes the impression was given that the new management wanted to get rid of everybody connected with the old management. In addition to Gus Van Sant, Bill Selden, and Fred Downey, they encouraged John Moriarty, the best sales manager in the company, who had spent his entire working life with Warner's and Warnaco, and Jim Gillies, vice-president for foreign operations, to retire as early as possible. But nowhere was the pressure greater than on Cameron Clark, former president. Walker and Lamoureux saw no place for him in their organization. In December 1977, I wrote Warnaco director, William Jennings, chairman of the Compensation Committee, "Cameron came to work for our Packaging Division in 1949. He was made president of Warner Packaging in 1959 and did an outstanding job. So much so that when we sold Packaging, we earned a very substantial capital gain, in the millions, for which Cameron must be given credit.

"Cameron is all that remains, along with me, of the team that built Warnaco. Jim and Phil stand to reap huge financial rewards, not only from their own efforts, but from the efforts of many people who went before them. The profits of today are coming from the divisions created yesterday by people like Cameron and me and so many others. We built the company soundly. It is ironic, and somewhat tragic too, that the ultimate rewards are not going to the builders, but only to those who restored profitability."

The appeal was useless. In a letter on June 27, 1978, I wrote Cameron to urge him to resign and do something else. "Jim and Phil are running this operation now for better or worse. They do not want you in their management councils. You have at least another ten years of active and productive business life ahead of you. For your own peace of mind and that of your family, these ten years should not be spent in an unhappy or frustrating atmosphere. . . . Make a clean break, Cam. Forget the past; forget the heartaches and the bitterness. Realize you did your best and call them bastards if you will, but look to the future."

Cameron took his own fate in his own hands and resigned from Warnaco to start an interesting business as a consultant in production sharing in Mexico, Central America, and the Caribbean. He has done well.

The era of Walker-Lamoureux was short-lived. In October of 1982 Phil stepped down from active management and was elected vice-chairman, a non-operating position he filled for only a few months before retiring. He said, "This move is in accordance with my original agreement when I moved into the operating management of Warnaco in 1976."

Jim Walker died unexpectedly on May 17, 1983, at the age of sixty-three from a kidney-related virus. The company and the whole apparel industry were shocked. He had just returned from a west coast meeting of the American Apparel Association, shortly after presiding over Warnaco's annual meeting at West Palm Beach. The menswear's trade paper, *Daily News Record*, wrote, "In his six years as Warnaco's C.E.O, Walker engineered the company's return to profitability and guided several of its divisions back to positions of dominance, particularly in menswear."

Fortunately for Warnaco a succeeding management was already in place. In late 1981 Robert Matura had been elected executive vice-president and Richard Kral senior vice-president/operations. Matura had started his career as a menswear buyer at Macy's and had subsequently been a vice-president at Hanes Knitwear in North Carolina and general manager of men's sportswear at Jockey in Kenosha, Wisconsin. He had joined Warnaco in early 1976 as president of Hathaway. Kral had spent most of his business life at Warnaco, becoming president of Warner's in 1976 after Lamoureux moved to corporate headquarters, and in 1980 had added the responsibility for Warnaco International. Immediately after Walker's death Matura was elected C.E.O. The board felt confident that in Matura-Kral it had a management team thoroughly competent and trained to replace Walker-Lamoureux. Unfortunately one part of this team was lost when a year later Kral elected to leave Warnaco to take over as C.E.O of the apparel division of General Mills, which was later spun off as a separate company under the name of Crystal Brands.

It was perhaps significant that in the year of Walker's death, 1983, the company's net income peaked at $28,342,000. With little spending on new products, promotions, advertising, production facilities, or personnel the balance sheet showed cash and accounts receivable alone exceeding total debt. In June the stock was split two for one, the dividend again increased, and the shares traded at an all-time high on the New York Stock Exchange.

Into the Eighties

15

The Middle Eighties

HE MID 1980s brought the years of the "big bucks," the era of personal greed. It started on Wall Street where speculators plotted megalithic corporate mergers, recapitalizations, leveraged buy-outs, friendly and unfriendly take-overs. It was more profitable for these traders to juggle ownership of companies than to concern themselves with the operation of those companies. Once staid investment firms made enormous fees by stirring up deals, while their employees, often young and inexperienced, amassed fortunes. Not to be outdone, corporate executives demanded and received much more in the way of salary, stock options, bonuses, "golden parachutes," incentives of all kinds. Many of them too seemed more interested in making a "deal," through which they could receive substantial sums of money, than with running their companies.

In such a climate fashion seemed completely eclectic, that almost anything went. But careful observers noticed that men and women were dressing to convey the image of what they conceived to be their own personal life-style, in extreme cases almost as if in a masquerade. Their clothes reflected what they thought of themselves and what they wanted the world to think of them, and they followed no dictates but their own. Women flocked to the job market; Liz Claibourne made a fortune designing simple, good-looking, inexpensive clothes for the working girl. Other successful merchandisers designed for a specific market, a specific life-style. The rule: know your customers, how they live, what they do at work and at play, what their dreams and aspirations are. Only then can you design for them. It was fatal to try to be everything for everybody.

By the time Bob Matura became president of Warnaco, he was pretty far removed from the changing world of fashions. Mostly that was up to the heads of the various divisions reporting to him, but, because he was a merchant, he *did* take a more active role in what the units were designing and selling than had Walker and Lamoureux, who were primarily concerned with financial results. Furthermore, Matura understood that his success and the company's success depended on continued careful watch of the changing life-styles of his customers.

As might have been expected, Warnaco's profits peaked with the 1983 results. Had Walker and Lamoureux remained on the job, their reputations might well have been diminished as profits declined. A company can be harvested only so long; tomorrow always comes.

Matura was fully aware that he faced a difficult assignment. He believed, as I did, that his predecessors had gone too far in their search for immediate profits, that they had drained the company of reserves, had neglected to build and plan for the future. Advertising and promotions had been minimized; personnel not added or trained; machinery required for increased production not put on line. Reduction in profits was inevitable if, once again, needed investments were to be made. As early as November of 1983, in his letter to the board submitting his 1984 budget, Bob commented on the need "to reinvest in our most important brands that are undernourished," and that "it would have been nice had we built up the funds necessary to finance our future rather than stretch for the earnings level of the last two years. . . . Since 1976 we have disposed of $200 million of assorted businesses. In order to survive this radical surgery we had to harvest our remaining divisions, particularly our primary brands. . . . This harvesting has hurt several of our brands. Our intentional direction of managing for the highest current earnings during the recent recession (mid 1981 to mid 1983) has caused a lack of momentum."

Matura realized that some of the money taken out of the company by Walker and Lamoureux would have to be put back. While once more building for the future, he would try to maintain the level of current earnings, but he knew this would be difficult and said so. "We are making selective reinvestments in our primary brands while trying to maintain the quality of our earnings."

I myself could work much more easily with Matura than with Walker, and, while not involved in any way in the operation of the company and no longer chairman, I remained a director until 1984 and after that an honorary director. Once more my counsels were asked for and listened to. Matura was a different kind of manager than Walker, somebody whose style of leadership I believed more suitable for a company like Warnaco. He was a hands-on manager, more salesman, bolder, anxious to build the company into something bigger and better. Had he remained president long enough to carry out his ideas, I believe Warnaco would have prospered.

In his first full year as president Bob tried to maintain the record earnings level while beginning to rebuild the company, but did not quite succeed. The first half profits of 1984 were ahead of the record set in 1983, but consumer spending took a sudden plunge, and retail stores were forced once more to cut inventories, built high in anticipation of business that never came. The inevitable result was substantial price cutting by apparel manufacturers, including Warnaco, in order to move *their own* inflated stocks. Total Warnaco sales increased 13 percent to $561,391,000, breaking the half billion mark for the first time, but after-tax profits dropped 28 percent.

In spite of disappointment, Matura remained convinced of the soundness of his policy of investment for the future. In 1984 he put through the company's first major acquisition since the troubles of 1976. This was the Olga Company of Los Angeles, a maker, like Warner's, of quality intimate apparel. Olga had been founded in 1941 by Jan and Olga Erteszek. He had been a lawyer in their native Poland; she was the daughter of a Krakov corsetier

Once more in the 1980s, as in the nineteenth century, Warnaco's was making lingerie, but with a difference.

Fig Leaves and Fortunes

and a refugee in the United States. To join her, Jan escaped through Russian lines just before the Germans invaded Poland at the start of World War II. Together in Los Angeles, they had nothing with which to start a new life in a new country except faith in each other and a determination to succeed.

Around the corner from their tiny apartment was a big department store, Bullocks Wilshire. In it, Jan and Olga saw their opportunity. For ten dollars they rented a sewing machine and bought a few yards of fabric, with which Olga designed a garter belt. Jan took the belt around to Bullocks Wilshire to see if they could sell it. They could, and did. The dozen garter belts Jan and Olga delivered to Bullocks sold out quickly, and they followed up with a girdle adorned with decorative flowers and bows. It too became an instant success.

In the years that followed, with Olga as designer and Jan as business manager, the company became one of the leading intimate apparel manufacturers in the country, known especially for the quality and femininity of its products. To bras and girdles were added daytime and nighttime lingerie and robes, and when their daughter Christine grew of age, she too joined the company as a designer. By 1984 the Olga Company had volume over $60 million and net profits above $3 million.

Olga had another distinction too. Jan considered himself fortunate to be in a country where entrepreneurship such as theirs could be so well rewarded, and he looked on his fellow-workers, not as employees, but as associates. In explaining his philosophy, he observed, "The concept of a hired hand of labor as a commodity is obsolete and incongruent with Christian teachings as they pertain to the dignity of man." He described his way of doing business as a "Common Venture" which sees "the employee as a person with needs beyond economic ones. It plans for employment as well as profit; it creates internal channels for redressing injustices. It recognizes that the modern corporation is not only a way of making a living, but it is also a way of life." To show belief in their own concept, Jan and Olga regularly contributed 25 percent of their pre-tax profits to their employee profit sharing plan.

Recognition for their philosophy of doing business came to Jan and Olga when their company was selected as one of "The Best 100 Companies to Work for in America," and when in 1984 they jointly received the award as "California Industrialist of the Year," the state's highest civilian honor, and the first apparel manufacturer ever to receive it.

This was the company Warnaco bought in June 1984 at a price of $28 million in cash. It proved to be one of the best investments it ever made.

Bob Matura faced another major problem in addition to the milking of assets by his immediate predecessors. By the decade of the eighties it seemed as if in America there were more rich and more poor. The victim of the social changes taking place was the middle class, the traditional bastion of American stability. Its size and influence waned in contrast to both the upper and lower economic classes. Important for Warnaco, this change was reflected among its customers in the retail world. The department stores, where the middle class shopped, lost share of market to the specialty stores at the higher rung of the economic ladder and to the discount stores at the lower. Some of the department store customers, rising in affluence, moved up to the higher-price specialty shops. Others dropped to the discounters. Fewer shopped at the department stores, which were caught in the middle with declining personal service for customers and a confused focus on what kind of stores they wanted to be. Such problems among department stores contributed, no doubt, to the

The Middle Eighties

Underneath fashion of the late 1980s. Where has the corset gone?

eventual takeover of many of them by speculators, who enriched themselves but, through the vast burden of debt incurred, caused the weakening and even the bankruptcy of some of their targets.

Department stores were hurt in another way also. It became fashionable, even among the wealthy, to shop both for unusual items and for bargains; it was the time of the so-called "smart shopper." This too helped the specialty stores, who had the skills to pinpoint a specific market niche, a specific lifestyle, and supply it with distinctive offerings, and also helped the discount stores with their low prices. To cope with the onrushing changes, each store or group of stores developed its own programs, many of which reflected adversely on the major brand apparel manufacturers such as Warnaco. To lower their costs and improve margins, retailers increased their imports. Sensitive to the charge of "sameness" in merchandise offerings, many stores embarked on private-label programs which offered not only lower costs and higher margins but so-called "exclusive" merchandise. Others went so far as to set up their own manufacturing or contracting facilities, thus blurring the distinction between manufacturer and retailer.

In a way, retailers were partially by-passing the national apparel brands. Having adopted their own importing, private label, or manufacturing programs, they were forced to give priority to those programs. Thus they tended to use the bulk of their open-to-buy for their own merchandise, to which they usually had to make commitments months, or even years, in advance. In turn they used the national brands, where they could get quick, at-once delivery, only to balance inventory—ordering if sales were good, withholding orders if sales were bad, and not ordering far in advance.

The only real weapon against all this for the manufacturer was the strength of his own brands. If a store was forced to stock a popular brand of apparel because customers demanded it, a manufacturer was still in control of his own marketing and his own destiny. Unfortunately Warnaco had not been strengthening its brands by promoting them; instead it had been taking profits out of them. What the company needed was to reposition and promote its brands in a major way in order to reestablish their strength in a time of change.

All of this would cost money and inevitably reduce profits, at least temporarily. Warnaco was a publicly-held company, listed on the New York Stock Exchange, and regularly followed by market analysts, whose reactions to even minor quarterly changes in the profits of any company could result in sharp ups and downs in the price of that company's stock—rises and falls often completely unrelated to the basic fortunes of the company. In view of what was happening on Wall Street, where avaricious hunters were on the prowl for under-valued "situations," what would happen to Warnaco if the price of its stock, after years of steady rises, should take a sudden fall? Would it be vulnerable to a take-over? Some of Warnaco's competitors, notably Levi, Blue Bell, and Palm Beach, worried about the same thing, had launched leveraged buyouts to repurchase their own stock and be able to plan their own future without outside pressure. Others, such as Cluett Peabody and Hartmarx, had failed to initiate their own action and had become targets of opportunistic investors.

What to do? Under the leadership of Chairman Matura, President Larry Pflieger, and Chief Counsel and Administrative Officer Lloyd Stauder, we began a series of research studies and discussions among our officers and with the board of directors on the future of the industry and of Warnaco. The objective was to determine the best way by which Warnaco could control its own destiny, not subject to the whims, changes, and policies

The Middle Eighties

The Olga Co., acquired by Warnaco in 1984, has a reputation for quality and femininity in its products.

Fig Leaves and Fortunes

of outsiders, whether of its retail customers or of Wall Street. All during the spring and summer of 1985 this study went on. Its pertinence was shown by the first half figures, which recorded a 25 percent drop in sales and profits from the year before. The sins of the Walker era were catching up with us; the need for doing something was apparent.

We had several alternatives:

1) We had the financial resources to diversify outside the apparel industry, thus minimizing the effect that changing retail patterns would have on the total company. However, this was not a popular course with either management or the board, both of whom felt that we would be incurring too many risks by moving into areas beyond our personal knowledge.

2) We could diversify into retailing. Theoretically at least, if we owned our own retail outlets, such as some combined retailers-manufacturers like the Limited were doing, we could be independent of other retailers. Certainly this combination was a developing phenomenon, but the difficulties were dramatic. It would be hard indeed for Warnaco to become vertically integrated by starting up, or acquiring, retail outlets without severely damaging its precious relationships with present customers. Besides the company had once tried retailing, albeit in a small way with Gus Mayer stores, and had not been successful.

3) We could be acquired by a large company outside the apparel field. In this way we would reward our stockholders financially, give them security, provide diversification to the company, and secure all necessary funds for whatever promotions and changes were necessary to strengthen our own brands. But currently apparel manufacturers were not in favor with large, diversified corporations. Cheseborough-Pond, Consolidated Foods, Gulf and Western, and General Mills had all recently sold, or spun-off, their apparel units. An offer from a large corporation to buy us was unlikely. Besides, management did not approve of the idea of losing its independence to an outfit that knew nothing about the apparel business.

4) We could continue to run the business as usual while looking for small, quality acquisitions within the apparel field, adjusting to change as much as possible without sacrificing existing market positions. Management and the board were against this idea because they felt that the accompanying necessity to maintain yearly earnings would not provide the resources to satisfactorily promote our brands or make other needed investments. The result, they feared, would be that the company would not achieve the growth in revenue and profits expected by investors.

5) We could acquire, or merge with, a very large company in the apparel field, such as Cluett Peabody or V.F. Together, such a combination with sales volume in the billions, would have the money and the market muscle to promote its products in a major way and not be dependent on the actions of the large retailers. This was the strategy I myself favored though management pointed out that the number of large apparel firms was severely limited and their interest or availability questionable.

6) Finally there was what management called the "repair and reinvest" strategy. The company had major needs. In addition to promoting its brands, its factories required investment to become lower cost producers. Key personnel had to be added and upgraded. Some units of the company should be dropped entirely, new ones added. All this would cost a large amount of money and, as previously mentioned, probably result in a decline in the price of Warnaco stock. Then the company itself could be vulnerable to a take-over.

Management believed that "repair and reinvest" was the preferred strategy, but how to go about it? It could be done either as a public company, or as a private concern after a buyout of the public stockholders. Remaining public, we would be vulnerable to a take-over, but as a private company, we would not have to worry about temporary drops in profit, and could afford to spend as much as necessary to build for the future.

During the summer I met with Matura, Pflieger, and Stauder to discuss my concerns about "going-private." I questioned whether becoming a private company solved our marketing problems. Granted we would have more flexibility to make moves without having to worry about short-term results in profits or stock price, but the cost of buying out the stockholders would be formidable indeed. Would it not leave us with so much debt that we would not have the resources to make the investments that had to be made? Matura responded that his projections showed that sufficient funds would be available for investment even after paying interest and principal on the inflated debt. I cautioned that projections of future profits and cash flows in the turbulent apparel industry were unreliable and had proved especially so at Warnaco. What if we had a severe recession or another sharp burst of inflation with rising interest rates? He insisted that the projections were conservative and believable. I was not convinced, but from the conversations I was aware that the three of them, Matura, Pflieger, and Stauder, were sure that "going private" was the best strategy. They had the solid backing of key members of the board, and I reasoned that it would be difficult for me, now only an honorary director without a vote, even if I felt strongly opposed, to persuade them otherwise. In addition, they were planning to include some fifty other Warnaco employees in their future ownership group and hence had the enthusiastic backing of their key executives.

In retrospect, I now believe I should have opposed their strategy more strongly than I did. Certainly, had their buyout gone through and the large, new debts assumed, they would have had to operate under constraints imposed by the banks and other financial supporters which would have made investments for the future difficult indeed. Furthermore, I am now sure that the proposed buyout put the company, as they say on Wall Street, into "play"— that it opened the way to a takeover, much more certainly than had we adopted the other strategy of simply letting the price of Warnaco stock fall as investments were made and profits dropped. There have been numerous examples of companies which have taken substantial reserves to solve existing problems without a major decline in their stock price or damage to their reputation. Matura did not agree with me, insisting that the buyout failed, not because the company was put "in play," but because the plan was not consummated quickly enough, as the lawyers dragged out arrangements, and that, even without the buyout proposal, takeover offers for the company would have come anyway.

Some observers and many old-time employees have been highly critical of Matura and his management group, claiming that they were relative newcomers to Warnaco and that they were operating, not for the good of the company, but for the substantial personal profit they expected to get from the deal. I am sure that this motivation was present, that, like so many many executives of their day, they were smitten by the "quick buck" fever, but I also believe that they thought they could benefit both the company and themselves through a leveraged buyout. They believed they could best operate Warnaco as a private company, out from under the public eye.

The regular October 1985 meeting of the board was held on the 25th of the month. After routine business, discussion centered on a "going private" strategy. Management said it had reached a decision to propose such a course of action and that it would like a special meeting of the board to do so. It was now obvious that the interests of management would differ from the interests of the stockholders, represented, as they were, by the outside directors. To satisfy this directorial responsibility and to act as advisor to the board, an independent committee of outside directors was appointed, headed by Aldo Papone, vice chairman of American Express.

To hear management's proposal the board convened in a special meeting five days later. Before the meeting, between October 23 and 29, the trading activity in Warnaco stock had accelerated sharply. Over the previous few years such activity had averaged 20,000 to 25,000 shares a day. It was now averaging 175,000 shares a day and the price had climbed from $23 to $27 per share. The day before the meeting a call had been received from the *Wall Street Journal* asking for comment on a rumor that Warnaco would be the subject of a leveraged buyout. That morning's *New York Times* also carried a report of the rumor, and there were statements on the Nightly Business Report of the Public Broadcasting System that the company was a takeover target.

With all this public attention some statement had to be made. The various alternatives were again discussed. I said I still had doubts about "going private," that it did not seem to solve our problems, and that I still believed that acquisition of, or merger with, another major apparel firm was the better answer. This would give us the muscle to steer our own course. Matura agreed in principle that this was a good idea but claimed it was impossible because there was no suitable partner to be found. He stated his preference for the "repair and reinvest" strategy and his belief that it could best be accomplished if the company were privately held. He pointed out that Warnaco was in the fashion business and hence was deeply dependent on the creative talents of its corporate and divisional managers. Private companies had an advantage over public ones in their ability to respond quickly to the market place and to retain, motivate, and compensate entrepreneurial talent. The buyout transaction to be proposed would help secure and retain such talent inasmuch as it would not be confined to the top echelon of management but would have a participation of some fifty corporate and divisional executives. Management-owners would be in control of the board of directors.

In a separate discussion, without management in attendance, the independent directors agreed that a "going private" transaction seemed to be in the best interest of the shareholders. They were advised by Sydnor Settle of the law firm, Simpson, Thacher, & Bartlett, that it would be necessary for them to engage a recognized investment banking firm, other than Goldman Sachs & Co., who was acting for the management group, to evaluate the fairness of any offer which might come from management. Mr. Papone proposed that Salomon Brothers Inc. be hired for that purpose, and his recommendation was accepted.

Management then re-entered the meeting, accompanied by representatives of Goldman Sachs. Matura and Michael Solovaara of that firm explained management's proposal. The stockholders would receive for each share a package of $27 in cash and $13 in principal amount of junior subordinated, 20 year discount debentures. The debentures would bear no interest for five years, then would pay 15 percent a year and be subject to mandatory redemption. The new term "junk bonds" was just at that time coming into general use, and everybody admitted that this was certainly a junk bond. Solovaara told the board that his firm believed this financing for the proposal would be available, that the future debt would not be too great for Warnaco to handle and, if necessary, to withstand an economic downturn, that cash coverage would be adequate, and that Goldman's projections had

The Middle Eighties

incorporated the "repair and reinvest" strategy and any additional investments required. The directors told Matura they would be prepared to recommend his proposal provided that Salomon submitted an opinion that it was fair to the stockholders and there was proof of the necessary financing.

Next day, as newspapers reported management's offer, Wall Street analysts valued the proposed debentures at $6 each, indicating they thought the package had a value of about $33 per share. Warnaco stock jumped to $30.125 on a volume of more than 500,000 shares. In a press interview Matura said he expected to preside over a private company by the end of the year. "We want to get off that ninety-day treadmill of earnings releases and market expectations and start investing and reinvesting in the company so that it's healthy twenty years from today rather than just three months from now. And by going private we will stay away from somebody who might want to take us over."

In both his time frame and ultimate objective, Matura was to be wrong.

16

Transition

DIFFICULTIES quickly developed with management's buyout proposal. Some long-time stockholders, as well as a few analysts, thought the price too low, that management was trying to steal the company. One analyst said, "You've got a jewel here. This company is well-managed, efficient, established. You've got a stable of brand names that is worth an awful lot. They've decided to save the company before somebody comes along and takes it from them." A couple of opportunistic law firms launched stockholders' suits against Warnaco's officers and directors. Richard D. Greenfield, attorney in one of the suits, was quoted as saying, "It's clear that the package of cash and junk bonds that the management is trying to force Warnaco shareholders to take is inadequate and unfair." Management's attorney called the lawsuits "typical" in situations like this, and added, "We do not believe the suits will impede the transaction."

More important were the problems Salomon Brothers was having with evaluating the fairness of the proposal. The usual method for such evaluation was to look at the offering price to see how it compared with the prior stock price, the existing book value, and the current multiple of earnings per share. By these standards management's offer fell in the median range of similar transactions. But Salomon could reach no quick opinion inasmuch as the details of the financing were still uncertain and because the value of the proposed debentures depended so heavily on the validity of management's projections of future sales, profits, and cash flow. If these projections were to prove too optimistic, the debentures would be worth little, or nothing. Without the proposed buyout Warnaco's balance sheet was formidably strong with cash and accounts receivable, all by themselves, covering almost all the debt. If the buyout was completed before year end, however, the balance sheet would show sharp deterioration. In my files I find a note written to myself. "I still believe the strategy of a major acquisition to be safer and better adapted to solving our marketing problems than this leveraged buyout. Maybe we should have tried harder to acquire Cluett instead of letting West Point have it. Some bankers I have talked to are

143

afraid of this amount of debt in a highly speculative industry. The company may well have to become smaller rather than larger. Units may have to be liquidated or sold to produce cash and reduce debt. Acquisitions will be impossible. Will this help solve the marketing problems? Will we have the money to tackle our major problems: restructuring, new production facilities, advertising, promotions, new ventures? And who is to say this whole thing will not produce an outside buyer?"

In order to forestall the possibility of such an outside bidder appearing with an offer to top theirs, management wanted to speed up the transaction. But the company counsel led by Sydnor Settle of Simpson, Thacher, & Bartlett, who was now representing the special committee of outside directors, felt it dangerous to hurry things. He did not approve of the structure for the transaction proposed by Goldman Sachs and Lawrence Lederman of the law firm of Wachtel, Lipton, Rosen, and Katz, counsel to management. They had suggested a novel form for the transaction consisting of a self-tender for Warnaco shares followed by a merger with RLL, the holding company created by the management group. This would have had the advantage of speed, but in the view of Settle and Ron Freeman of Salomon contained legal and regulatory problems. They preferred a more standard or "plain vanilla" structure based upon an S.E.C. approved proxy solicitation of Warnaco stockholders. After considerable discussion the directors' committee told management it thought it preferable to go ahead with a "plain vanilla" merger even if it took more time. Matura and his group reluctantly agreed, but blamed Settle for the length of time involved, which ultimately, they believed, cost them their deal.

By the middle of December, with a "plain vanilla" structure agreed upon, most of the other difficulties had been overcome as management modestly increased its offer by agreeing to pay 16 percent interest on the debentures instead of 15 percent and having them mature in sixteen instead of twenty years and with the General Electric Credit Corporation making a commitment for financing. These agreements enabled Salomon to provide a firm opinion that the management proposal was fair to Warnaco stockholders and also permitted a settlement with the litigating stockholders and their lawyers.

On December 19, 1985, the board of directors unanimously approved the agreement with management and recommended that it be accepted by the shareholders. A meeting for that purpose was set for March 21, 1986, later postponed to April 18. To Warnaco's management, and others, this seemed a long wait, but a lengthy proxy statement and details of the proposed financing consumed much of the time.

On March 17 a bomb dropped on Warnaco. On that day the board of directors received an offer from W. Acquisition Corp. to purchase for cash all the company's common stock at $36 per share.

WAC was a newly-formed Delaware corporation established for the purpose of acquiring Warnaco. Its most important principals were Andrew G. Galef and Linda J. Wachner. The Warner's division of Warnaco knew Linda well. Back in the middle seventies she had been a highly successful vice-president of that division in charge of advertising and promotions. She was a graduate of the University of Buffalo, with a degree in business and economics, and began a retailing career as an assistant buyer at the Associated Merchandising Corporation, then moved on to Foley's in Texas. Next she became the foundation garment buyer at Macy's, New York. She was at Macy's when Phil Lamoureux hired her for Warner's.

Shortly after her relatively brief stint at Warner's, she was employed by David Mahoney, the chief executive of Norton Simon Inc., who was impressed by her abilities and her determination to succeed. He appointed her president of Max Factor, the large cosmetic company owned by Norton Simon. It was there she made her reputation as a brilliant operator, turning a $16 million loss into a $5 million profit in two years. It was at Max Factor also that she first attempted to fulfill her ambition of owning and running a company. In 1984, when Norton Simon was bought by the Beatrice Companies, she tried to get control of Max Factor through a leveraged buyout. When this did not work, she resigned. Then, with the backing of the investment firm of Adler & Shaykin she pursued the beauty business of Revlon, Inc. In early 1986 she was thwarted there too as Pantry Pride acquired the whole of Revlon and did not want to part with any of it.

Linda's new associate was Andrew Galef, a California investor and founder of the Spectrum Group, a management firm specializing in acquiring, improving, and selling small businesses. Early in the battle over Warnaco Galef announced that if they were successful in taking over the company, he would become chairman and Linda, president and chief operating officer. In other words, Linda would run the company. Together they believed that Warnaco was a great treasure but that it was not being run as well as it could be. They were convinced that with Linda as president it would more fully realize its potential.

The Warnaco board met on March 21 and again two days later to consider the WAC offer. Since October, when management had first proposed a leveraged buyout, there had been dramatic changes in the financial markets and in Warnaco ownership. Interest rates had fallen sharply and stock values risen. Ten-year Treasury Bills were down to 13.5 percent while the Dow-Jones was up 16 percent. Accordingly, the interest rate of 16 percent in the management offer now looked too high. In addition, the old, conservative families and institutions which had for so many years owned Warnaco stock no longer did so. From December on, 85 percent of the company's shares had changed hands. Many of the former stockholders, attracted by the increasing price of Warnaco stock, had cashed in their holdings at a substantial profit. The purchasers of these shares had been speculators betting that in a buyout or takeover the price would go even higher. Now 50-70 percent of the shares were held by arbitrageurs and a large part of the rest by new-to-Warnaco institutions. For these new stockholders there was no loyalty to the old company. For them there was only one criterion: the price. They would sell to the highest bidder.

At the board meeting, Bob Matura recalled that he had first become aware of the interest Linda had in Warnaco when, along with Galef and Jeffrey Deutschman, a partner of Galef's, she had visited him in January of 1985 at his office in Bridgeport. They had told him then that they wanted to discuss the possibility of acquiring the company through a leveraged buyout with management participation. He had told them he had no interest.

It was obvious by now that whoever was going to run Warnaco in the future was going to have to do so under the burden of heavy debt. The opinion of the board was that the current, experienced management was more capable of doing this than newcomers, no matter how capable. Therefore the members believed it was their responsibility to do everything in their power, within the limits of legality and financial prudence, to defend against any unsolicited offers.

To do this, management and Goldman, Sachs put together a plan to recapitalize the company. First, the management takeover would be dropped. In view of the financial changes in the market, and now the offer from WAC, it was obsolete anyway. In its place would be a proposal to issue new notes, stock, and cash to shareholders, who would receive for

Transition

each share of current stock at least $7 in cash, notes with a face value of $29, and stock in a recapitalized Warnaco that would be equivalent to slightly less than 80 percent of their current holdings. Warnaco officers and employees would increase their percentage of ownership from 5 percent to 29 percent. The value of the package was put at $41 per share by the company but analysts considered its worth about $39 per share or around $400 million in total. In any case it appeared to be superior to the WAC bid of $36. A stockholders meeting was set for April 25 to approve management's new offer.

As is usual in such cases, suits and counter-suits were the first results of the conflicting bids. Warnaco sued WAC for what it saw as the tender offer's violation of federal security laws involving takeovers. WAC sued Warnaco and its directors for violation of security laws, for not giving consideration to WAC's bid, and for "not giving shareholders enough information to make an informed decision." But the lawsuits were a sideshow. Everyone knew that the principal game was in the bidding.

On Sunday March 30 WAC raised its offer from $36 per share in cash to $40. Wall Street, thinking the bidding would go still higher, jumped the price of Warnaco stock to over $42.

As the bidding grew more tense, acrimony between the two sides increased. Galef was quoted as saying, "We are disappointed that the [Warnaco] board of directors, rather than meet with us, chose to waste the company's time and money on defensive litigation, poison pills, and an unsound recapitalization plan designed to entrench and enrich certain members of senior management." He added, "It's a super company, but it's undeveloped in marketing and product. We don't think they have capitalized on the franchises they have." He also charged that the company had tried to stifle competition among bidders for Warnaco shares by authorizing "golden parachutes" for top executives and confusing the public about the WAC offers.

In turn, Matura claimed that Galef and Wachner did not have the experience to run an apparel company the size and complexity of Warnaco. "We can do it better," he insisted.

Attention of the financial world was now focused on the struggle. An article in *Business Week* claimed Warnaco was trying to be its own "White Knight," and that it was using the first "real junk bond defense." Goldman Sachs described it as a "public leveraged buy-out." An article in the *Wall Street Journal* reported cynicism among some anaylsts about the motivation of Warnaco management in first offering to buy the company for $33.30 per share in a leveraged buy-out, then offering much more when pressured by the WAC bids. One analyst said that management still wants "to be in control of the situation" and figures "this is the best way to do it." Warnaco's management justified the increase in price by the changes in the financial markets, including the rise in the stock market.

There was one important consideration involving Connecticut law. This law held that a recapitalization such as Warnaco was proposing was illegal if, after the transaction was completed, the fair market value of the company's assets was less than its total liabilities. In one of its suits against Warnaco, WAC had charged that the company's liabilities, plus the debt incurred to finance its recapitalization, would exceed its total assets. Based upon "book value," this was true, but the law was based on "market value." Warnaco's management believed that the fair market value of the company's assets exceeded its proposed liabilities, and in fact had received from the American Appraisal Company a preliminary opinion that the market value of those assets *did* exceed such liabilities.

The Warnaco board met on April 2 to consider the increase in WAC's offer to $40.00 per share. It was the opinion of both Salomon and Goldman, Sachs that the current Warnaco price amounting to between $39 and $41 per share, was highly competitive to the increased WAC bid, and was fair to shareholders. D. F. King, the company's proxy solicitor, was reported as saying that the company's recapitalization plan was considered by Wall Street as superior to the WAC tender offer of $40. The proxy for the proposed April 25 meeting was just about to go out. Lawrence Letterman of Wachtell, Lipton, who was advising on strategy, suggested that before doing anything, the company should monitor reactions to the proxy materials. He pointed out that the company's shares were now held by sophisticated investors, who would reach quick conclusions and that we would soon know how they would vote. It was further reported that through Manufacturers Hanover Trust Company the company had obtained necessary financing for the recapitalization.

Just before the next board meeting on April 7, WAC offered $42.50 cash for a merger agreement, an offer clearly superior to the company's. Whether the board and Warnaco management could legally increase its own bid to top WAC's now depended on the fair market value of the company's assets. Present at the April 7 meeting were representatives of the American Appraisal Company, whose opinion would be crucial. They outlined the scope of a detailed appraisal which they had made of the company's assets and reviewed the facilities which they had visited. It was their opinion that total assets should be marked up by $210 million to reflect fair market value, enough of an increase to allow a modest improvement in the price offered shareholders, if the board wanted to make any such increase. On the basis of these figures, management recommended that the company's offer be increased from $7.00 to $9.00 cash per share and $30.00 in notes and debentures, plus one share of the proposed new common stock. The total value would be about $44 in contrast to WAC's $42.50.

A long discussion followed as to the advisability of making this increased offer. Management reported that under the financial arrangement with Manufacturers Hanover there were adequate funds to cover the debt and the inevitable negative cash flow for some years to come. Director Robert N. Anthony, Professor of Management Control, Emeritus, at the Harvard Business School, questioned the American Appraisal figures and declared he could not support the revised recapitalization proposal, because, in his judgment, its debt involved more risk to the company than he thought prudent.

It was not an easy question for the board to decide, and there was considerable difficulty on the part of each director in making his decision. In the end they felt the risk tolerable and the advantage to maintaining ownership and control considerable. Dr. Anthony, however, said that he thought he had been wrong in his earlier votes in favor of the recapitalization and, now that he was opposed, had decided to tender his resignation from the board. The board accepted his resignation, and then unanimously approved the increased offer.

WAC responded quickly. On April 14 Galef wrote a letter to the Warnaco board increasing their offer to $44 per share in cash and announcing that they were filing proxy material with the S.E.C. in opposition to the recapitalization plan, on which a vote was expected at the stockholders meeting, now only eleven days off. In his letter he quoted an opinion from the judge at the United States District Court who had denied Warnaco's plea for an injunction against WAC's tender. "Management's self-interest rather than its fiduciary duty may well be a motivating factor here, at odds with the interests of shareholders and more self-serving than altruistic." In the board's opinion this was not a fair

Transition

accusation. Management still believed that because of their experience and knowledge of the company and of the industry they could run the company better than Wachner and Galef. And it was a fact that the Warnaco officers would benefit far more personally if the company was taken over than if the recapitalization was successful. If they were dismissed by a new management, the proxy of April 4 estimated Matura would receive $5,609,198 in terminal pay; Pflieger, $2,540,041; Stauder, $1,129,167; and Arthur Warshaw, a vice-president, $1,787,351. In addition they would receive the profits from the sale of their stock and presumably payment for unexercised stock options.

In a letter to Warnaco stockholders, Galef was bitter. He assailed the board for the proposed increase in debt, for the reduced stockholders equity, for the operating loss which would be incurred, for the golden parachutes of the executives, for some proposed amendments to Warnaco's certification of incorporation that would dilute voting rights of substantial shareholders, even for the original management-led leveraged buyout which he declared was "grossly underpriced."

Warnaco was now a company under seige. On April 17, only eight days before the scheduled stockholders meeting, its board met again. Matura suggested there were three alternatives. First, take no action and let the marketplace decide between the value of the company's recapitalization proposal of about $44 per share and the competing WAC $44 cash tender offer. Second, increase the company's bid by $1.00 in cash. Third, try to find a "White Knight" to enter the bidding, though at this late date and at this high price, such an alternative seemed unlikely. Management favored the $1.00 increase which they believed would make its proposal once more superior to WAC's.

The board again spent a long time in serious consideration. In the opinion of many members the proposed debt was already much too high, and WAC, backed up by their investment bankers at Drexel, Lambert, seemed determined to take over the company no matter what the price. Again the board was advised that any increased bid would be legal only if the members, with the advice of experts and in the exercise of their considered business judgment, were able to revalue the company's assets to a fair market value which would permit the company to remain solvent. Management insisted this was true; the board agreed and voted for the $1.00 increase. But it knew that this was as far as it could go; it was at the end of the line. If WAC topped this price, the battle was lost.

On the eve of the April 25 scheduled shareholders meeting, WAC *did* top it. Galef wrote a letter to the Warnaco board and issued a press release announcing that they would be prepared to increase their bid to $46.50 per share in cash if 51 percent or more of the outstanding Warnaco shares were "validly tendered and not withdrawn, and the tendered shares represent, in the judgement of WAC, sufficient shares . . . to defeat the Warnaco recapitalization plan."

For Warnaco, it was all over. There was no way it could meet a $46.50 cash offer. To do so would be financially foolish and probably illegal. Because it knew it would lose the shareholder vote, the company early on April 24 postponed the meeting set for the next day.

That evening communication was established with WAC, and negotiations begun between Matura and Galef and the necessary lawyers and financial advisors on both sides. The meetings lasted all night. Finally a merger agreement was reached giving WAC control of Warnaco. Subject to board approval, the agreement included: 1) settlement of all litigation; 2) all shareholders to receive $46.50 cash; 3) Andrew G. Galef and Linda J. Wachner to be elected chairman and president respectively; 4) existing employment, consult-

Fig Leaves and Fortunes

ing, stock options, and retirement agreements to be honored; 5) all other contractual rights to be protected.

It was a good agreement, especially for the top Warnaco officers, who were liberally rewarded for the coming loss of their jobs. On Friday April 25, the Warnaco board of directors met for the last time. It was a sad meeting. Matura explained what had happened over the previous few days. With the help of the $1.00 increase which the board had approved, the price of Warnaco stock had risen to close on Wednesday April 23 at $44 7/8. Proxy solicitors had been making good progress in getting votes favoring the management recapitalization plan, and it looked as if the company might win the Friday vote. On Thursday morning, however, came the WAC offer of $46.50. The Warnaco offer could not be increased to compete. The professional traders would vote for Galef, Wachner, and company. Also there was no last minute "White Knight" in view, who might be persuaded to get into the bidding. The price had simply gone too high. Somebody noted that in the twenty-five years since 1961, when the company first went public, the value placed on Warnaco by the financial world had increased from $16 million to the $487 million now being paid by WAC.

Sometime around six on that Friday evening the board approved the merger and adjourned. It was a beautiful spring evening in New York, but the beauty did not lift our spirits. For some of us who had lived through so many years and so much history with Warner's and Warnaco, there was special pain. It was 126 years since the little wagon had left the hamlet of Lincklaen carrying Lucien Warner to riches and moderate fame. There had been so many up years and so many down years in all the time since, so many men and women, now remembered only as ghosts of the past, who by their hard work and devotion had made the company what it was. Through all those years it had been *our* company, something almost as personal, and as precious, as our families. But now it was no longer *our* company. On Monday morning, there would still be a Warnaco, and hopefully a vigorous and profitable Warnaco, but it would be owned and managed by somebody else.

Transition

Illustrations and Credits

The illustrations which appear in *Fig Leaves and Fortunes* came from a variety of sources and the author is deeply grateful to all those who so generously provided assistance. The uncaptioned illustrations which embellish the chapter titles were assembled by the author from various printed materials over an extended period of time and identification of original sources is simply not possible.

All captioned illustrations are listed in the order in which they appear and the abbreviated title is followed by the source and, where known, the appropriate photographic credit. In the following, the Fairfield Historical Society is abbreviated FHS and the Bridgeport Library Historical Collection BLHC. Material from both corporate and divisional sources within Warnaco are so designated and the miniature photos of corporate principals appearing in the front matter all came from corporate sources or from the author.

Index

Index

Index

FIG LEAVES AND FORTUNES

has been published in a first edition
of twelve hundred copies.
Designed by A. L. Morris,
the text was composed in Paladium
and printed by Knowlton & McLeary
in Farmington, Maine on Monadnock Caress Text.
The jacket and endleaves were printed on Strathmore Grandee Text,
and the binding in Holliston Mills Roxite
was executed by New Hampshire Bindery
in Concord, New Hampshire.